The Alaska-Siberia Connection

TEXAS A&M UNIVERSITY

48

MILITARY HISTORY SERIES

The Alaska-Siberia Connection

The World War II Air Route

By Otis Hays, Jr.

Texas A&M University Press
College Station

The paper used in this book meets the minimum requirements
of the American National Standard for Permanence
of Paper for Printed Library Materials, Z39.48-1984.
Binding materials have been chosen for durability.

Maps provided by Cartographic Service Unit of the
Department of Geography at Texas A&M University

Library of Congress Cataloging-in-Publication Data

Hays, Otis, 1915–
    The Alaska-Siberia connection : the World War II air route / by
Otis Hays, Jr.
        p.   cm. — (Texas A & M University military history series ;
48)
    Includes bibliographical references and index.
    ISBN 0-89096-711-3
    1. World War, 1939–1945—Aerial operations, American.   2. World
War, 1939–1945—Aerial operations, Soviet.   3. World War, 1939–1945—
Transportation.   I. Title.   II. Series.
D790.H3895   1996
940.54'4973—dc20   96-17489
                                                              CIP

For my cheerleaders,
Sonny and Patricia and Judy and Gordon

Contents

Illustrations

Preface

Two hundred years after Vitus Bering made his Siberian connection with Alaska in 1741, the German invasion of the Soviet Union in 1941 set the stage for a renewed Alaska-Siberian connection during World War II. An expansion of the U.S. Lend-Lease program held together an unlikely Soviet-American alliance. Various seaborne and airborne routes funneled vast amounts of Lend-Lease supplies and military equipment, including aircraft, to the embattled Soviet Union (chap. 3).

The Alaska-Siberian (ALSIB) Air Ferry Route[1] was one of the funnels. Fifty-six percent of the Lend-Lease aircraft that reached the Soviet Union war front flew over the ALSIB route in 1942–45.[2]

The Army Air Force's Air Transport Command ferried factory-new airplanes from Great Falls, Montana, across Canada to Fairbanks, Alaska, over the Northwest Staging Route.[3] Red Air Force pilots with the Soviet Military Mission at Fairbanks began the relay of the aircraft from Alaska across Siberia.

In 1942–43, the relationship between Americans and Soviets in Alaska presented challenges to build and maintain confidence of one for the other. Unforeseen problems were frequent. Although liaison personnel were fluent in each other's languages and dedicated, misunderstandings could and did occur. Undercurrents of suspicion were always present. Later, secrecy and rumors of intrigue clouded the story of the three-year Alaska-Siberian aerial reconnection. However, progressive international cooperation ensured the success of the ALSIB route's mission. American and Soviet airmen shared subarctic flying hazards in which men died. They surmounted most of the divisive language and cultural barriers. They refused to allow mutual mistrust overwhelm them.[4]

As a member of the Alaska Defense Command's military intelligence staff and as supervisor responsible for Soviet liaison activities, I was aware of the ALSIB story as it unfolded.

Most of the Alaska-Siberian reconnection story, from the ALSIB route's birth to its development into an effective Soviet-American Lend-Lease delivery system, came from three main sources of primary information: military intelligence files, liaison officers' recollections, and Russian contributors.

A search of the National Archives records located the Alaska Defense Command/Alaskan Department's 1943–45 weekly military intelligence (G-2) reports. Specialized annexes were integral parts of many of these intelligence documents. One group of annexes contained "Russian Information Reports" from Nome and Fairbanks, Alaska.[5] Another group of annexes addressed either "USSR Personnel" or "Foreign Liaison (Russia)."[6]

Former American liaison officers who served at Fairbanks and Nome provided a second body of essential information, their reminiscences furnishing many details not previously available. They included George G. Kisevalter of McLean, Virginia, the first chief liaison officer at Fairbanks, in 1943–44; Michael B. Gavrisheff of Silver Spring, Maryland, liaison officer (later chief liaison officer) at Fairbanks, 1943–45; David Chavchavadze of Washington, D.C., interpreter at Fairbanks, 1943–44, field-commissioned to become liaison officer at Fairbanks, 1944–45; and Igor A. Gubert of Oakland, California, liaison officer-in-charge at Nome, 1943–45.

Russian sources made other valuable contributions to the story. Among the contributors were Elena Makarova, Peter Gamov, Victor Perov, and Aleksandr Kotgarov, all members of the ALSIB section of the Soviet War Veterans Committee in Moscow, Russia; Silvio Sclocchini of Irkutsk, Siberia; and the editors of *Soviet Life* and *Russian Life* in Washington, D.C.

In addition, valuable reminiscences, photographs, assistance, or encouragement came from Adm. James B. Russell, USN-Retired, Tacoma, Washington; from several Alaskans, including John H. Cloe, Chief of History, Eleventh Air Force, Elmendorf Air Force Base; Edward J. Fortier, retired executive editor, *Alaska* magazine, Anchorage; Richard R. Hoopes, Randy and Marion Acord, and L. D. ("Corky") Corkran, Interior and Arctic Alaska Aeronautical Foundation, Fairbanks; Edward A. Long, Fairbanks; Robert N. DeArmond, Juneau; Kay Shelton and the staff of the Alaska Historical Library, Juneau; and from Joseph Kerns, Tucson, Arizona; James A. Ryan, Bakersville, California; Louis B. Klam, Warner Robins, Georgia; Cecelia and Theodore Suchecki, Milton, Massachusetts; Hans-Heiri Stapfer, Horgan, Switzerland; Michael Schneider, Washington, D.C.; and Cindy Frazier and her library staff, Monett, Missouri.

The Alaska-Siberia Connection

1.
Connection
and Disconnection

The prehistoric Bering land bridge during the Ice Age was the first Siberian connection with Alaska. Using it, Siberian animals crossed to Alaska and Asian hunters, ever in search of food, migrated in waves to North America. Forebears of native Alaskans arrived in later migrations.[1]

The recorded history of the Alaska-Siberian neighbors began less than three hundred years ago. The original Russian connection across Siberia and the Bering Sea with Alaska (1741–1867) endured until Russia sold Alaska to the United States. During the resulting Alaska-Siberian disconnection (1867–1941), the ambitions and confrontations of Russia and Japan in the Far East delayed any reconnection until the World War II ALSIB route reunited Alaska and Siberia once more.

In 1581, cossacks penetrated the Ural Mountains and seized a Russian tochold on the west fringe of Siberia.[2] The booty of conquest was fur, including luxurious sable, mink, and ermine pelts, all in great international demand. As word of fur-rich Siberia spread, cossacks, trappers, and traders poured eastward and pushed thousands of miles across the vast Siberian wilderness.[3] The Siberian tribesmen were subdued and forced to pay *yasak* (tribute in fur). The imperial tax collectors exacted the czar's share, also in fur.[4]

The Russians moved relentlessly across Siberia, leaving fortified *ostrogs* (outposts) along the way.[5] In a single human lifetime, they reached the eastern shores of Siberia at the Sea of Okhotsk in 1639.[6] At the same time, the reckless Russians intruded in the Amur River valley along the northern border of the Chinese empire. Chinese troops drove them out. Finally, in 1689, a Sino-Russian treaty signed at the Siberian village of Nerchinsk denied any Russian claim to the Amur River basin and blocked Russian expansion in the Far East for 170 years.[7] Backing from the Amur region, venturesome Russians reached the Kamchatka Peninsula and, in 1696, looked upon the icy (Bering) sea and the empty eastern horizon beyond.[8]

Only days before his death in January, 1725, Czar Peter I ("the Great") signed an imperial order directing extensive exploration and scientific research in Siberia and in any adjacent unknown lands. He was especially interested in Russian discovery of a possible land connection between Siberia and North America. The czar selected the Danish-born Vitus Jonassen Bering, a retired Russian navy officer, to undertake the task.[9]

The expedition headed by Bering and his lieutenant, Aleksei Chirikov, eventually reached Kamchatka's eastern shores and, after building a seagoing ship in 1728, sailed to chart the Siberian coast to the north.[10] They sailed through the Bering Strait as far as Cape Dezhnev (East Cape).[11] Unable to see mainland America to the east, Bering returned to his Kamchatka base convinced that Siberia and America were not joined and that he had fulfilled his mission. In 1728–30, he made the arduous journey to St. Petersburg and reported his finding to the imperial court.[12]

Bering soon planned a second Siberian expedition that gained approval in 1732.[13] More than nine years passed, however, before he attained the ultimate goal of his plan, that of sailing eastward to America.

In June, 1741, Bering and Chirikov in two new ships, the *St. Peter* and the *St. Paul*, departed Bering's Kamchatka base, Petropavlovsk. Storms soon separated the two ships.

Six weeks later, Bering observed an Alaskan mountain range from the Gulf of Alaska, after which he ordered the *St. Peter* to set a return course to Petropavlovsk. Upon reaching the Bering Sea, the *St. Peter* was dashed on unchartered Bering Island. The crew escaped ashore but Bering and thirty-one of his men died during the winter.

Meanwhile, Chirikov in the *St. Paul* found land two days before Bering's sighting but to the southeast. The *St. Paul* returned to Petropavlovsk in early October, 1741. In the summer of 1742, the *St. Peter*'s survivors built a small vessel from their ship's wreckage on Bering Island to take them to Petropavlovsk.[14]

Bering's expedition discovered more than new Russian territory. It revealed an unrivaled source of priceless fur—the pelts of sea otter and fur seal—in the Aleutian Islands and adjacent waters. The Aleutian natives—Aleuts—had migrated to the islands at least seven thousand years before.[15] At the time of Bering's expedition, the combined Aleut population, skilled in hunting with kayak and harpoon, was about ten thousand.[16]

News of the fur bonanza spread rapidly in Siberia. As a result, Russian traders sponsored by Siberian commercial companies quickly arrived and forced the Aleuts to hunt for them. The Aleuts tried to resist.[17] Subjugated and their numbers reduced to about two thousand by terror, massacre, and disease, the surviving Aleuts did the Russians' bidding. After the source of fur dwindled in the Aleutian Islands, the Russians relocated Aleuts to hunting waters elsewhere.[18]

Grigorii Shelikhov, an ambitious merchant from Irkutsk, formed a company that established the first Russian colony in Alaska. In 1784, despite native Aleut opposition, he personally settled the colony on Kodiak Island.[19]

After he returned to Irkutsk, Shelikhov selected Aleksandr Baranov as his colony's new manager. Baranov sailed for Kodiak in 1790.[20] A group of Russian Orthodox missionaries[21] and additional settlers reinforced the colony in 1793.[22]

Shelikhov died unexpectedly in 1795 and his son-in-law, Nikolai Rezanov, assumed control of Shelikhov's interests in Siberia and Alaska. In 1799, Czar Paul I granted a charter for Rezanov and his stockholders to operate a fur-trading enterprise, the Russian American Company, the nucleus of which was the earlier Shelikhov company.[23]

At Rezanov's urging, Czar Alexander I and members of the imperial court became stockholders in the Russian American Company.[24] For as long as Russia owned its Alaskan connection, the Russian American Company remained Russia's exclusive agent.

Aleksandr Baranov had absolute authority over Shelikhov's colony and the successor Russian American Company. He steadily planted fur-trading outposts eastward along the rim of the Gulf of Alaska as far as Sitka.[25] Baranov moved his headquarters to Sitka where, beginning in 1805, it became the center of political, economic, and military activities in Russian America.

The Achilles' heel of Baranov's operation proved to be the colony's food situation. His farming experiments in Alaska were unsuccessful.[26] He was forced to trade with foreign ship captains, especially Americans, for supplies.[27] He sent ships to California and Hawaii to trade for basic foodstuffs and even established a Russian farming outpost, Fort Ross, in California.[28]

Baranov retired in 1818, thereby giving the Russian navy an opportunity to leave its mark on Russian America. A series of ranking navy officers, commoner as well as aristocrat, entered the service of the Russian American Company to manage its operations.[29]

In 1821, the czar banned all foreign ships from Alaskan waters and extended Russia's territorial claims along the Pacific coast to Vancouver Island. The czar's action helped to spur the American 1823 pronouncement of the Monroe Doctrine and the 1824 Russian-American treaty that, in effect, canceled Russia's Alaskan maritime restrictions and plans for territorial expansion.[30]

At the peak of the Russian American Company's operations, the Russian population in Alaska numbered less than one thousand. Over half of the Russians in the colony lived at Sitka.[31] Most of the company's employees were offspring of Russian fathers and Alaskan native mothers and were recognized officially as "creoles." Their number in company service neared two thousand.[32] The propagation of Russian surnames among the descendants of the creole population became one of the legacies of Russian America.

By 1855, the near extermination of the sea otter had put the Alaskan fur-trading glory days of Baranov beyond recall. Because the future of the Russian American Company was bleak, Russia's disposal of Alaska soon was a matter of negotiation.

Nikolai Muraviev, the new governor general of Eastern Siberia, wanted to hasten the demise of the Russian American Company. Soon after his appointment in 1848, he argued for Russian withdrawal from Alaska. Instead, he wanted Russian official attention directed to Russian expansion in the Far East.[33]

Muraviev's ambitions were temporarily set aside by Russia's involvement in the Crimean War (1854–56). Enemy British and French fleets mounted attacks on Muraviev's Siberian domain, but the results were insignificant except for the British destruction of the village at Petropavlovsk.[34] The war did not touch Russian America itself.[35]

Although Russia lost the Crimean War, Muraviev quickly resumed his enthusiastic pursuit of Russian expansion into the maritime regions that China had long denied to Russia. When he found that the weakened Chinese were incapable of resisting, Muraviev boldly moved Russian settlers into the coveted territory. He planted two new mushrooming settlements, Khabarovsk on the lower Amur River (1858) and Vladivostok, a year-round ocean port (1860). Shortly thereafter, the 1860 Treaty of Peking fixed the new Chinese-Russian border as being east and west along the upper Amur River and south along the Ussuri River.[36]

Influencial Russian navy and finance officials at St. Petersburg adopted Muraviev's earlier notion of Alaskan disconnection and convinced the czar to offer Alaska for sale to the United States.[37] Secret negotiations were delayed, however, because the United States government was preoccupied with the outbreak and course of the Civil War.

The 1860s also saw an attempt at Russian-American connection. For the first time, a transcontinental telegraph line linked New York and San Francisco in 1861, and the Russian government planned to build a telegraph line across Siberia to connect the Russian Far East with Europe via St. Petersburg.

Cyrus Field of the American Telegraph Company had failed at several attempts since 1857 to lay an Atlantic submarine cable to Europe. Hiram Sibly of the Western Union Telegraph Company, assuming that Field's future efforts were also doomed to failure, decided to construct a telegraph line from America to Russia and Europe via the Bering Strait. The route of the planned line passed through western Canada and Russian America (Alaska), across the Bering Strait via submarine cable, and then through northeast Siberia to connect with the Russian trans-Siberian line.[38]

Three separate construction crews were dispatched in 1865: one to Canada, another to Alaska, and the third to Siberia. Then, without warning, the project collapsed in July, 1866, when Field at last laid a working trans-Atlantic cable. The crew in Canada learned the news immediately—Field's announcement flashed over the four hundred miles of completed telegraph line. The two isolated crews in Alaska and Siberia, however, waited a year until July, 1867, to be located and told that their labor was for nought.[39] Had the project been completed, the century-old Alaska-Siberian connection would have been perpetuated literally by a thread—the cable across the Bering Strait.

In February, 1867, United States and Russian representatives resumed the delayed negotiations for the sale of Alaska, and they signed the treaty for the $7.2 million purchase on March 30. Russia ratified the treaty on May 15, and the U.S. Senate, influenced in part by the publicity generated by the Alaska-Siberian telegraph project, ratified it on May 28.[40]

Dmitrii Maksutov, a navy officer and hereditary Tatar prince, was the last manager of the Russian American Company.[41] Login O. Gavrishev, another senior navy officer, served as the company's assistant manager.[42] Gavrishev, also remembered as Russian America's last lieutenant governor, was brother to the great-grandfather of Michael B. Gavrisheff, one of the key American foreign liaison officers on the ALSIB route during World War II (chap. 5).

Maksutov and Gavrishev were unaware of the secret negotiations to sell Alaska. Without warning, Maksutov suddenly received orders to release his Russian-American domain to its new owners, the United States government. The historic transfer ceremony was conducted according to ritual at Sitka on October 18, 1867. However, the subsequent confusion among Russian citizens and the disputes over company property created a period of chaos. Matsutov arranged passage for all Russians, including his own family, who wished to return to Russia. After finishing the lengthy, painful task of liquidating the company's assets, Maksutov himself departed Sitka fifteen months later, in January, 1869. His departure marked the end of Russian America and severed Russia's Alaska-Siberian connection.[43]

In 1884, as though to emphasize the Alaska-Siberian disconnection, a world concord adopted an international date line to standardize a global calendar. The imaginary line extended through the Bering Sea and the Bering Strait, separating Alaska from Siberia by an artificial time gap of an entire day.[44]

As the nineteenth century neared its end, the fur harvest on the Siberian coast continued to beckon American entrepreneurs from Alaska. Ships of fur traders ranged the Siberian coastal villages during the short ice-free seasons. Russian officials tolerated the American intrusions by selling legal trading permits and using patrol boats to intercept illegal operations.[45]

Following the emancipation of Russian serfs in 1861–63, Russian emigration had added millions to Siberia's population. Pressure for economic and social development in Siberia called for the construction of a railroad to unite the empire. Surveys were begun in 1885 for a single-track railroad from the Ural Mountains to Irkutsk and across the Stanovoy Mountains and the Transbaikal to Vladivostok.[46]

Undeterred by the abandoned telegraph project across Alaska and Siberia in the 1860s, American promoters dreamed of building a railroad to Alaska. In 1891 while Americans still dreamed, the Russian government acted. Approved by the czar, construction of the Trans-Siberian Railroad commenced.[47]

The czar's approval immediately awakened American businessmen to the economic opportunities in Siberia and the Orient in general. Several of them, including railroad magnate Edward Harriman,[48] believed that a railroad tunnel under the shallow waters of the Bering Strait was feasible. Their daring proposal envisioned a railroad net from Alaska through the tunnel to connect with the Trans-Siberian Railroad. The proposal gained serious support until Czar Nicholas II in 1907 denied American railroad entry into Siberia.[49]

By then Russia had already come up against the Japanese. American Adm. Matthew Perry had aroused Japan from her medieval isolation in 1853–54 by securing American trading rights—an agreement that opened Japan's doors to wider foreign contacts, including with the Russians. Japan and Russia were early rivals for possession of Sakhalin Island and the Kurile Islands. The rivalry was settled in 1875 by a treaty that confirmed a negotiated trade: Sakhalin Island to Russia in exchange for the Kurile Islands to Japan.[50]

Japan watched while Russia used the Trans-Siberian Railroad to penetrate China's Manchuria. When railroad builders reached Chita, east of Lake Baikal, Russia obtained a Chinese concession for a shortcut railroad across Manchuria, thereby saving hundreds of miles on the rail route to Vladivostok. The resulting Chinese Eastern Railroad was completed in 1903.[51] China also agreed to lease Port Arthur on the Liaotung Peninsula to the Russians, a concession that gave Russia access to a warm-water port free of winter ice.[52]

Russia's progress in emerging from Siberia, however, ran counter to Japan's interest in Manchuria and Korea. The inevitable Russo-Japanese war erupted in early 1904 with a surprise Japanese navy attack on Port Arthur. Besieged by sea and land, Port Arthur surrendered in January, 1905.[53] Meanwhile, the czar ordered the Russian Baltic fleet to the Far East. The six-month voyage ended in May, 1905, in the Tsushima Strait, where the combined Japanese fleet encountered the Russian fleet and destroyed it.[54]

Unable to funnel timely reinforcements across Siberia by railroad and beset with revolutionary unrest at home, Russia accepted the reality that the war was over. By the Treaty of Portsmouth in 1905, Russia lost Port Arthur as well as the lower half of Sakhalin and recognized that southern Manchuria and Korea were in Japan's sphere of influence. Russia, however, retained its interest in the Chinese Eastern Railroad within a northern Manchurian buffer zone for the next thirty years.[55] The region was thoroughly Russianized.[56]

In 1916, despite overwhelming obstacles caused by World War I and domestic upheaval, the Russian government completed the construction gaps in the main Trans-Siberian Railroad from Chita to Vladivostok.[57]

A year later in 1917, the Bolshevik Revolution ignited four years of bloody civil war that pitted the revolutionary Red Army against the counterrevolutionary White Army. The 1918 Treaty of Brest-Litovsk removing Russia from World War I marooned tens of thousands of Czechoslovak ex-prisoners of war who had fought for the Allies on the Eastern Front. The men, referred to as the "Czech Legion," offered to continue fighting Germany on the Western Front. The Legion's only feasible route to Western Europe was via the Trans-Siberian Railroad to Vladivostok, where evacuation ships waited.[58]

In June, 1918, a portion of the Legion arrived at Vladivostok but the main body was confronted and trapped at Irkutsk by Bolshevik armed forces and their supporters. The Czechs appealed to the Allies for help. In August, President Woodrow Wilson ordered two regiments of American troops to Vladivostok to cooperate with Japanese forces in "rescuing" the Czechs. The American soldiers were deployed along the Trans-Siberian Railroad between Vladivostok and Lake Baikal.[59]

Meanwhile, the civil war raged across Siberia. White Army forces under Adm. Alexander Kolchak enjoyed early successes near Omsk in 1919. As winter approached, however, they collapsed. Kolchak fled from Omsk toward Irkutsk in a convoy of trains with $300 million in Russian government gold. At Irkutsk, Kolchak surrendered to the Czech Legion. The Czechs, wanting only to escape to Vladivostok, delivered Kolchak to the Bolsheviks in exchange for safe passage from Siberia. The American-assisted evacuation of the Legion through Vladivostok began in February, 1920. The American troops followed, the last soldier leaving Vladivostok in April.[60]

After Kolchak's White Army debacle, Russian cossack Gen. Grigorii Semenov's independent army continued to resist the Red Army in Eastern Siberia.[61] Soon, however, countless refugees and remnants of defeated White Army units, including Semenov and some of his men, crossed the border to find haven in Manchuria.[62]

After they established diplomatic relations in 1924, China and the recently created Soviet Union agreed that they would jointly operate the Chinese Eastern Railroad, although China recognized too late that the agreement was a mockery.[63] With the Soviet Union in control of the railroad, hostility between the White Russian and Soviet factions in Manchuria was inevitable. The atmosphere in the two opposing camps remained tense for the next decade.[64]

The Bolshevik victory in Siberia ended any Japanese hope for early expansion into former Russian territory. Instead, Japan turned again to China. In 1932, Japan occupied and converted China's Manchuria into a Japanese puppet state, Manchukuo. Confronted with Japan's unrelenting pressure, the Soviet Union in 1935 finally surrendered its last foothold in Manchuria by selling its share of the Chinese Eastern Railroad to Manchukuo's puppet government for a fraction of its worth.[65]

The Manchurian loss occurred in the midst of the Soviet Union's urgent efforts to meet domestic economic goals set in a series of five-year plans, beginning in 1928, with the use of the *gulag* (corrective labor camp) system.[66] Throughout the 1930s, heavy industry was massed along the Trans-Siberian Railroad corridor and along the Amur River from Khabarovsk to the river's mouth. Although gulag camps were located in the rich mining areas of Kamchatka and Chukotski, the region facing Alaska escaped heavy industrialization.[67]

After World War I, the pioneering days of flight began to tie the Bering Sea neighbors in new ways. After World War I, the arrival of the "air age" thinned the curtain that separated the Bering Sea neighbors. The process by which the airplane connected remote Alaska with the continental United States was a slow one, but one that also led to the eventual reconnection of Alaska with Siberia by airplane.

Soon after the war, military aircraft in two dramatic demonstrations brought attention to Alaska's strategic location in relation to the Far East. The first was the 1920 flight of four army planes from New York to Nome and back.[68] The other was the daring 1924 flight of four army "round-the-world" aircraft via Alaska.[69] Inevitably, adventuresome bush pilots followed the military trailblazing in Alaska. Of the many bold bush pilots, one man especially—Ben Carl Eielson—became an early legendary figure.[70]

Despite drastic Soviet restrictions on American commercial operations with Siberian natives, veteran trader Olaf Swenson obtained fur-trading rights from Soviet officials. In 1929, Arctic ice trapped one of Swenson's fur-laden ships northwest of the Bering Strait. Hired by Swenson, Eielson vanished while flying from Alaska to retrieve the furs. A joint Soviet-American search lasted two months until the wreckage of Eielson's airplane was found on the Siberian coast and his body recovered.[71] Although Swenson's subsequent withdrawal from Siberian trading operations effectively ended American commercial contact with Siberia, the joint international quest for Eielson was the beginning of a series of American and Soviet cooperative aviation ventures in the decade to follow.

In 1931, Charles and Anne Morrow Lindberg surveyed an aerial route to the Orient via Alaska and Kamchatka.[72] Two years later, Jimmy Mattern crash-landed in Siberia during his failed round-the-world flight. He was flown to Alaska by Sigismund Levanevsky, one of the Soviet Union's pioneer aviators.[73] In 1935, two world-famous Americans, Will Rogers and Wiley Post, planned to cross Siberia en route to Europe. They died when their plane crashed near Point Barrow.[74]

Meanwhile, Soviet airmen used Siberia as a proving ground for cold-weather testing and endurance flying. Later, they launched three separate demonstration long-distance polar flights to North America in the summer of 1937. In June, Valeriy Chkalov flew from Moscow to Vancouver, Washington.[75] In July, Mikhail Gromov established a long-distance record for nonstop flying—6,300 miles from Moscow to San Jacinto, California.[76] In August, Sigismund Levanevsky departed Moscow with Fairbanks as his announced destination. He never arrived. An international search found no trace of the missing plane.[77] The Soviet Union's continued interest in long-range aircraft resulted in the purchase of a Glenn Martin four-engine flying boat in 1939. Dubbed the "Russian Clipper," the flying boat entered service in the Soviet Far East in 1940.[78]

Military considerations gained currency only gradually, although as early as 1934, Lt. Col. H. H. Arnold (later World War II chief of the Army Air Forces) had led a mass flight of bombers to Alaska and assessed army aviation defense needs. He recommended to his Washington superiors that an air base be located at Fairbanks. As year after year passed, Congress repeatedly failed to provide construction funds.[79] By contrast, the civil aviation picture was brighter. Landing strips and four airfields (Juneau, Anchorage, Fairbanks, and Nome) became the backbone for coastal and interior Alaskan routing of early commercial airlines, and weather and navigation services were promised.[80]

By 1939, Japanese military aggression was unabated in China and Manchuria.[81] The outbreak of war in Europe awakened the Canadian government to the need for more and better airfields in the airmail route corridor from Edmonton via Fort St. John to Whitehorse. Concerned U.S. and Canadian defense planners realized that improved facilities for the rapid movement of military aircraft across western Canada to Alaska were essential.[82] Congress at last voted the necessary funds for the Fairbanks air base (the future Ladd Field). Construction commenced immediately and continued through the winter of 1939–40.[83]

German armies rampaged through Europe in 1940, leaving the Netherlands East Indies and French Indo-China in Southeast Asia without protection from their subjugated European mother countries. Japan eagerly turned her attention to the vast stores of strategic raw materials found in the vulnerable region. Because the military-dominated Japanese government ignored American protests regarding Japan's aggressive moves toward Southeast Asia, President Franklin Roosevelt ordered a selective embargo on exports to Japan.[84]

With Japanese-American relations continuing to deteriorate in 1940, Congress rushed funding authorization for an operational air base at Anchorage (the future Elmendorf Field), navy base facilities at Sitka, Kodiak, and Dutch Harbor, and deployment of army ground forces to Alaska. Army Col. Simon B. Buckner, Jr., was selected to develop and command the new Alaska Defense Force.[85] Knowing that time was late, Buckner recommended that a fan of military bases be established to protect, in order of priority, the Bering Sea approaches, the three navy bases, and the coastal air route between Seattle and Anchorage. He also formed an alliance with Marshall Hoppin, the Civil Aviation Administration (CAA) manager in Alaska, many of whose civilian airfield projects fitted into Buckner's concept of Alaskan defense.[86]

2.
Reconnection
by Air

Reacting to German as well as Japanese aggression, President Roosevelt alerted the American public to the dangerous situation that now existed in a world being consumed by war. Especially alarmed by Germany's lightning conquests in Europe and the isolation of Great Britain in 1940, he called for American rearmament. He mobilized the military services and the arms industry to expand their capabilities for the defense of the nation.[1]

Desperate Great Britain made cash purchases of American-made arms. Roosevelt, however, realized that funds of the besieged island defenders were limited. He therefore proposed to share American arms production and supplies with Great Britain and other nations threatened by would-be conquerors. He introduced his proposal, called "Lend-Lease."

The president presented the Lend-Lease legislation to Congress with the argument that military aid should be provided whenever the defense of any country was considered to be vital to the defense of the United States. After extensive debate, the Lend-Lease Act was passed and the president immediately signed it into law on March 11, 1941.[2] The act eventually benefited thirty-two nations.

During the debate, unsuccessful efforts were made in both houses of Congress to deny the extension of Lend-Lease aid to the Soviet Union in the event of war. Roosevelt, also aware of the degree of public hostility toward the Soviet Union, therefore knew that any offer of Lend-Lease support to Moscow would depend on future developments.[3]

A month after the passage of the Lend-Lease Act, the Soviet Union and Japan signed a neutrality pact of five years' duration. The two governments agreed to the treaty for different reasons. Although the Red Army was considered to have won the 1938–39 border clashes with Japan's Kwantung Army, the Soviet Union was currently involved with developing events in Europe. Moscow therefore wanted to reduce Soviet-Japanese tensions in the Far East. Japan, by softening its stance against the Soviet Union in Siberia, now was able to concentrate on seizure and exploitation of strategic resources in Southeast Asia.[4]

On June 22, 1941, despite international intelligence warning Moscow of an impending invasion of the Soviet Union, German armed forces successfully launched a massive surprise attack on unprepared Red Army defenders.

From the time when the United States and the Soviet Union established diplomatic relations in 1933, the relationship had been cautious and tainted with suspicion. To Americans, the Soviet Union represented the seat of communism, both hated and feared in America. On the other hand, Soviets regarded U.S. actions during the Red Revolution as having been hostile, and they remained convinced that the Americans wished only ill for the communist experiment.

In 1939–40, the already careful attitude of Americans toward the Soviet Union took a major downturn. This now was the Soviet Union that had signed a nonaggression pact with Nazi Germany, sliced off the eastern portion of Poland, annexed the independent Baltic states of Latvia, Lithuania, and Estonia, and invaded Finland—hardly the record expected of a possible future military ally.[5]

Yet, on June 22, 1941, these were desperate times. The U.S. government had already committed itself to aiding the beleaguered Great Britain and China through Lend-Lease. After the Soviet Union's battered Red Army was reported to be reeling before the invading German juggernaut, the U.S. government quickly decided that a tentative program of military assistance to the Soviet Union was in the national interest. The key question was whether the Red Army was sufficiently capable and determined to resist the invaders.

Soviet Ambassador Constantine Oumansky in Washington at first was uncertain about the American reaction to the critical situation confronting the Soviet Union. However, after the State Department reassured him on June 26 that the United States would favorably consider any Soviet request for aid, Oumansky on June 30 presented a list of emergency supplies and equipment, both military and industrial. Oumansky's positive outlook and his list left no doubt of the Soviet Union's determination to fight. One of the major requests on the list was aircraft—three thousand fighters and as many bombers. Oumansky said that some of the short-range bombers could be flown from Alaska to Siberia by way of the Aleutian Islands. The airfields in Siberia were in excellent condition, he said.[6]

Before the Soviet request could be evaluated, the War Department became alarmed by the speed with which the German military formations were advancing against the crumbling Red Army resistance. Gen. George Marshall, U.S. Army chief of staff, sensed the possibility that Japan might take advantage of the Soviets' disarray and overrun the Soviet Far East. On July 3, he placed the army forces in Panama, Hawaii, and Alaska on alert.

In Panama and Hawaii, the reaction to the alert was generally satisfactory. In Alaska, however, the alert revealed serious weaknesses in Buckner's emergency patchwork defense system. Communications were among the first flaws to appear. The undermanned Alaska Communication System (ACS) required four days to notify the various military outposts. In addition, Alaska lacked the capability of detecting the approach of enemy aircraft or ships. In the absence of any operational early warning radars and navy patrol aircraft, Buckner ordered his handful of B-18 bombers from Elmendorf Field to Nome for the purpose of patrolling the Bering Sea.[7]

Remedies for the uncovered weaknesses commenced. The ACS soon was geared for wartime operations and the construction of early warning radars was accelerated.[8] The navy in July started deployment of two patrol squadrons to the Alaskan navy air stations at Sitka, Kodiak, and Dutch Harbor.[9] When it became obvious that Japan's Kwantung Army was remaining behind its border fortifications in Manchuria, General Marshall canceled the alert. Buckner, however, kept his B-18 bombers on Bering Sea patrol until September.

Determined to secure Southeast Asia even at the risk of certain war with the United States, Japan on July 25 proclaimed a joint Franco-Japanese protectorate over Indo-China. The United States, Great Britain, and the Netherlands reacted immediately by freezing all Japanese assets and imposing a total trade embargo. The U.S. government was aware that the accelerating drift into war could be stopped only by Japan's agreement to withdraw from Southeast Asia, which was not likely.[10]

In Washington, one of the critical arguments within the government concerned the distribution of the military aircraft coming off the new American assembly lines. The problem was how to divide the available aircraft for meeting the needs of the American armed forces as opposed to fulfilling the major Lend-Lease allocations to Great Britain and China. President Roosevelt's promise of aid to the Soviet Union presented a further problem. He wanted to deliver aircraft as token reassurances of American commitment in order to inspire continued Soviet resistance to the German invasion.

During July and into August, the War Department argued against trying to ferry aircraft from Alaska across Siberia, as Ambassador Oumansky requested, because of inadequate airfields and facilities. But the Soviet ambassador continued to insist that the airplanes could successfully complete the flight. During this argument, the Soviets' aircraft requirements and arrangements vacillated in number, type, and delivery route.

In mid-August, the on-again, off-again negotiations called for diverting fifty-nine P-40 fighters from a British Lend-Lease allocation and then sending them, plus five B-25 bombers, to Alaska where Soviet crews would meet them. This arrangement, like previous ones, did not hold. The Soviets' change of mind asked for the fighters to be shipped to Archangel and Soviet crews to be trained for flying the B-25s to the war front via Newfoundland and Ireland.

Then, in late August, Oumansky announced the newest plan, this time again involving Alaska. Bomber crews were being sent to the United States via Alaska for training.[11]

On August 31, General Buckner's B-18 bombers from Elmendorf Field were on patrol over the Bering Sea. Three of the bombers were covering sectors west and northwest of Nome. James A. Ryan was Lieutenant Fillmore's navigator. Ryan recalled that Fillmore's bomber encountered two PBY Catalina-type flying boats bearing the Soviet Union's red star insignia. For some reason ("Perhaps they were lost," Ryan said), the two flying boats landed first at Kotzebue north of Nome but were aloft again when Ryan saw and photographed them. Under escort, the two Soviet craft landed at Safety Lagoon (Nome).[12]

The senior Soviet officer in charge was Gen. Mikhail Gromov, the same Gromov who had established the long-distance endurance record on a flight from Moscow to California four years earlier, in 1937. As one of the Soviet Union's veteran military airmen, Gromov was applying his experience to yet another pioneer flight. This time, fellow Soviet airmen comprised his cargo, and by careful planning he crammed forty-

Soviet-built PBY flying boat as it approached the Alaskan mainland from Siberia on August 31, 1941. Photograph by James A. Ryan

seven into the two aircraft. Starting from Moscow on August 28, the two loaded flying boats flew to Archangel and, on August 29 and 30, across northern Siberia to Anadyr. From there they crossed the Bering Sea to Alaska.

At Nome the exhausted Soviet airmen rested. A Russian-speaking Orthodox priest volunteered to act as interpreter. On September 1, the Soviets awakened and learned that Anatoly N. Felotoff, an attaché from the Soviet embassy in Washington, was coming to Nome aboard a commercial airline flight. Felotoff arrived hours later as scheduled, bringing documents authorizing the Soviet airmen legally to enter the United States.[13] On September 2, the rested Soviet airmen reboarded their flying boats and flew to Kodiak.

Lt. Comdr. James S. Russell had arrived at Kodiak Naval Air Station in mid-July with Patrol Squadron VP-42. Russell's unit was equipped with PBY-5 Catalina flying boats of the type that became famous during

World War II. He vividly recalled the overnight visit of the Soviet airmen who were en route to Seattle.[14]

Russell's instructions were clear: Welcome the Soviets, service their aircraft, and send them to the Sitka Naval Air Station the next morning. The Soviet flying boats, although built in the Soviet Union, were similar to the PBY flying boats used by Russell and his squadron.[15]

The two visiting aircraft were scheduled to arrive at 5:00 P.M. on September 2.

"On the evening of their arrival," Russell said, "officers of the air station and my squadron assembled on the seaplane ramp. . . . Suddenly, and at exactly five o'clock, both planes appeared overhead. They made good landings and good beach approaches. . . . With our beaching gear attached, the two Soviet Catalinas were hauled to parking spots on the concrete apron."

Although ladders were immediately put in place to allow the passengers to disembark, nothing happened, Russell said. Finally a Soviet general (who later introduced himself as Mikhail Gromov) appeared and asked permission to land his party. After Capt. Jack Perry, commander of the air station, responded, the occupants climbed from the two crowded planes on signal.

Finding emergency accommodations for nearly four dozen visitors proved to be a problem, especially since the top floor of the officers' quarters, still under construction, could house only a few. However, cots with mattresses and linens were moved to an adjacent barracks for the others.

Responding to Russell's request that Gromov speak to the base and squadron officers that evening, Gromov gave a truly fascinating talk, Russell said. Gromov described his Moscow-to-California flight achievement in 1937, summarized the aviation progress in the Soviet Union, and analyzed the military situation on the Soviet-German front. Then he abruptly changed the subject and voiced his disapproval of the design of the naval air station. His unexpected criticism was the forerunner of other personal disapprovals he later expressed after he arrived in Washington.

Although they were tired, the Soviet flyers were restless, and some of them attended impromptu parties. Later in the night, Russell was awakened by a knock on his door. An agitated Soviet officer, waving his arms wildly, met Russell when he opened his door. The officer claimed that he was insulted because he was billeted in an enlisted men's barracks. After trying to explain that a military base under construction had limited sleeping space, Russell invited the furious officer to take his own bed, and Russell prepared to vacate the room. Suddenly sobered by Russell's reaction, the Soviet officer retreated.

In the meanwhile, the squadron intelligence officer, on Russell's instruction, examined the two parked Soviet-built flying boats. The hasty investigation confirmed, Russell said, that both aircraft had been stripped in order to carry the passenger overload. Only those instruments and equipment that were absolutely essential to operate and navigate the craft remained. All armament and armor had been removed, and even the specialized gear needed for beaching the flying boats had been eliminated. To save weight and space, Gromov and his crews had gambled on the availability of compatible American beaching gear at Kodiak and later at Sitka and Seattle. The Soviets' radio equipment, however, was intact, so Russell would have no trouble in maintaining contact while the visitors were over U.S. waters.

Early the following morning, September 3, the Gromov group squeezed into their planes. The prescribed launching was executed without flaw, and the visitors were quickly airborne.

While they were crossing the Gulf of Alaska, the Soviets reported by radio that a submarine had been sighted. "This sent us to the plotting room. The submarine was neither one of ours nor a known friendly," Russell said. "We manned all of our Catalinas present at Kodiak [at that time, five] and searched the area. We found nothing." Russell added that the submarine was aware that it had been sighted and, as a result, was well hidden below the surface when Russell's squadron arrived.

Gromov's party arrived at Sitka as scheduled, and on September 4 continued to Seattle. According to Seattle news reports, the plans of the Soviet aviators remained almost as much a mystery as had been their surprise arrival at Nome five days earlier.[16] At the same time in Washington, the War Department announced that a Soviet military mission en route to the United States via Nome was purely a technical one. According to the War Department spokesman, the mission members would observe the operations of American aircraft plants.[17]

The Soviet airmen—bomber crews and technicians—were delivered to Spokane, Washington, to begin their training on B-25 bombers that they were planning to fly to the Soviet Union. At Seattle, the two Soviet flying boats began a return flight through Alaska to Siberia.[18] When they arrived at Kodiak to overnight, Russell's intelligence officer again inspected them while they were parked in Russell's squadron hangar. This time, Russell said, each flying boat was loaded to its maximum gross weight limit, not with human cargo but with belted machine gun ammunition.

At Spokane, the Soviet bomber crews were eager to begin their training but, taking their cue from General Gromov,[19] were critical of the B-25 bombers. Gromov went to Washington and conveyed his complaints directly to General Arnold himself. Gromov insisted that his men were entitled to better aircraft, such as the B-17, the heavy bomber then in production. Arnold firmly rejected the request for the heavy bombers. He told Gromov that the B-17 was not suited for Red Army-style ground support, and that the Army Air Forces were unable to share any of the B-17 production for months to come.

In mid-September, Gromov dismissed the B-25 as unsatisfactory because it lacked armor, gun turrets, and the range necessary for the flight to the war front. Gromov and Andrei Gromyko, Soviet chargé d'affaires, were invited to inspect a later model B-25 and a B-26 bomber on display at at Washington's Bolling Field. They decided to accept a combination of both types of medium bombers. These aircraft, they said, should be readied to fly to the Soviet Union by October 5. Meanwhile, the bomber crews at Spokane were brought to Patterson Field, Ohio, for training.

But the indecision was not yet over. On October 1, the Soviets rejected the B-26 as unsuitable for combat. Since they still doubted that the B-25 had sufficient range for the long flight home, they decided that the bombers should be sent via water transport. Then, on October 3, they asked that the bombers be equipped for de-icing. The disruption and confusion from changing Soviet requirements meant further delay, but eventually five B-25s were shipped to the Soviet Union in November.[20]

Although the first U.S. bombers destined for Soviet use were thus not flown to the Soviet Union, the historic Alaska-Siberian reconnection by air in both directions had already been accomplished without fanfare by the round-trip flights of the two Soviet flying boats between August 31 and mid-September, 1941, setting the stage for establishment of the ALSIB route a year later.

3.
ALSIB
Route Plans

The birth of the ALSIB Lend-Lease route was a lengthy ordeal with complications. On the one hand, the Soviets knew from the beginning of American aid that an ALSIB route could provide a rapid flow of urgently needed aircraft to the battle front. However, the ALSIB route had to be remote from the southern border of the Soviet Far East in order to be as far from Japanese attention as possible. On the other hand, the United States searched for ways to deliver supplies and weapons, especially aircraft, to ensure the survival and potency of the Soviet armed forces. The War Department persistently proposed that American airmen could ferry combat aircraft to the Soviets in Siberia. By furnishing such a ferry service, the Army Air Forces hoped to gain access to air bases in Siberia for future use.[1]

The battered Red Army had suffered severe losses in the early weeks after the German invasion of the Soviet Union. American public opposition to helping the Soviet Union began to decline, and soon more and more Americans endorsed the sale of arms to support the defenders. Still, isolationists in Congress continued to attack the Soviet Union and introduced new resolutions to bar the Soviet Union from participating in the Lend-Lease program.[2]

Although Ambassador Oumansky assured the president that the Red

Army was not on the brink of collapse, Roosevelt wanted a firsthand appraisal of the situation. He sent his special assistant, Harry Hopkins, as his personal envoy to talk with Stalin in Moscow.

In mid-August of 1941, Roosevelt and Winston Churchill held their historic Atlantic Conference aboard warships off Newfoundland. Harry Hopkins returned from Moscow in time to join the meeting. He reported that the Red Army, crippled as it was, could and would fight, but it required substantial military aid before undertaking any counteroffensive. Among the decisions emerging from the conference was agreement for a joint mission to go to Moscow for the purpose of assessing the Soviet Union's critical defense needs.[3]

Arriving in Moscow in late September, Averill Harriman, the Lend-Lease coordinator to Great Britain, headed the American delegation and Lord Beaverbrook the British one. They met a cool, suspicious Stalin. Despite the initial tensions, however, the meeting produced an arms supply agreement identified as the Moscow Protocol and signed by the United States, Great Britain, and the Soviet Union.[4]

Roosevelt, sympathetic from the beginning to the Soviet Union's request for assistance, used weeks of careful political and budgetary shadowboxing with the Congress until late October, when the Congress passed the second (renewal) Lend-Lease appropriations bill.[5] Shortly thereafter, the president declared that the defense of the Soviet Union was vital to the defense of the United States, and the Soviet Union promptly became a priority member of the Lend-Lease family on November 7.[6]

Accelerated U.S. arms production still fell far short of American defense needs. Nonetheless, the U.S. government was determined to honor its commitment to the Soviet Union. Difficult though making the decision to share American arms production had been, finding the means of delivery to the Soviet Union was just as difficult.

The Soviet merchant marine fleet itself was too small for the task. The extraordinary demands and casualties of war immediately caused a worldwide shortage of Allied ships. However, both the United States and Great Britain agreed to provide as many cargo ships as possible for Lend-Lease delivery service.[7] Three main supply routes were employed in the early efforts to meet delivery schedules.

The shortest route was the direct one to the Soviet Arctic ports of Murmansk and Archangel. This so-called North route was also the most dangerous. Ship convoys, usually assembled near Iceland, ran a gauntlet of German air, surface, and undersea attacks in the Arctic Ocean off northern Norway. The convoys later endured losses so severe that they were temporarily suspended for periods in 1942, 1943, and 1944 but were resumed at great risk.[8]

The longest route was across the southern Atlantic Ocean and around Africa's Cape of Good Hope to the Persian Gulf. Whether by surface or air, the Persian Gulf route depended on passage through Iran to the Soviet Union. In 1941, shortly after the German invasion of the Soviet Union, British and Soviet forces jointly entered and occupied Iran. The pro-German shah was deposed. With a cooperative young Mohammed Riza Pahlavi placed on the throne, Iran then became the funnel—known to the Soviets as the South route—for the movement of Lend-Lease aid by road, rail, and air to the Soviet Union. However, due to the initial lack of adequate port, highway, and railroad facilities, the south route via the Persian Gulf did not become a reliable and high-volume avenue for Lend-Lease supplies until 1943.[9]

A third and most productive route crossed the North Pacific and passed through Japanese waters via the La Perouse, Tatar, or Tsushima straits to reach Vladivostok and other available Siberian ports where Soviet ships discharged their Lend-Lease cargoes. The burdened Trans-Siberian Railroad net dispersed the cargoes westward. Despite Soviet-Japanese neutrality, the Soviets' ships were at risk, especially when they approached their passage through the Kurile Islands. Nine vessels were sunk. Soviet ships augmented by reflagged Lend-Lease freighters and tankers nevertheless successfully delivered approximately half of the overall Lend-Lease tonnage from the United States to the Soviet Union on the trans-Pacific route.[10]

Two additional but minor Lend-Lease routes were later established. One was the arctic route via the Bering Strait used in the summers of 1943–45 to reach Siberian Arctic ports with supplies for the ALSIB route air bases. The other was the Black Sea route used in 1945 to move supplies through liberated Soviet ports.[11]

In the beginning, the delivery of Lend-Lease aircraft was a time-consuming process. The planes were disassembled, crated, and loaded aboard freighters. On arrival at a debarkation port, they were off-loaded and then reassembled for final delivery. Lend-Lease fighters and light bombers were urgently needed at the war front in the shortest possible time, and ship-borne delivery alone was not satisfactory. Ferrying bombers over the long aerial route via the South Atlantic Ocean, North Africa, and the Middle East was feasible, but even that partial solution did not allow the United States to meet scheduled deliveries as promised. The logical air ferry route for volume deliveries was the shorter one through Alaska and Siberia. The operation of such a route was on the minds of both Soviet and U.S. leaders in 1941–42.

As frustrated American officials discovered during the course of the war, Soviet-American collaboration was not an easy accomplishment. Gen. John R. Deane, chief of the United States Military Mission to Moscow (1943–45), described the situation in his postwar report: "Soviet officials have an inherent [historical] distrust of foreigners and may be expected to examine for a hidden motive any proposal for collaboration. This will always result in indeterminate delays. . . . This [search for hidden motives] applied even to those cases where Americans were attempting to provide the Soviet Union with supplies and equipment that would benefit the war effort."[12]

Although they welcomed the prospect of American Lend-Lease assistance, the cautious Soviets were nonetheless suspicious about American motives and determined that the Lend-Lease program not be implemented in such a way that the Japanese could use it as a pretext to renounce the Soviet-Japanese Neutrality Pact. Fear of a premature war with Japan, therefore, was an obstacle to an early agreement for an ALSIB connection. Limitations later imposed by the Soviets on the future ALSIB route's operations reflected their concern. As a result, the wary Soviets repeatedly rejected all collaboration proposals that would allow American presence in Siberia.

In the flurry of initial negotiations for the emergency delivery of American-made aircraft to the Soviet Union, it was Soviet Ambassador Oumansky who had insisted that the planes could be flown from Alaska via Siberian airfields to the war front. The War Department had brushed the idea aside.[13] However, intrigued by the possibility that American pilots could deliver aircraft to the Soviets at airfields in Siberia, the War Department asked Oumansky for information on all trans-Siberian airfields and their weather reporting and communications facilities.[14] Although the request was not fulfilled, this early evidence of American interest in Siberian bases did nothing to stifle Soviet suspicions and may have delayed agreement to open the ALSIB route.

During Averill Harriman's visit to Moscow in late September, he discussed with Stalin the question of using Siberian air bases to deliver American aircraft from Alaska. Stalin showed some interest in the ALSIB route, but he objected to the suggestion when Harriman mentioned that American airmen might be used to ferry the aircraft across Siberia. The ALSIB route, Stalin responded, was too dangerous. The subject was not pursued.[15]

Both the North and South routes were yet to be tested as satisfactory avenues for the delivery of aircraft, but the Soviets secretly still considered that an ALSIB route mentioned by Oumansky in Washington was worth serious investigation. An ALSIB route would permit aircraft to be ferried battle-ready to the war front in a matter of days. Anticipating the need for this shorter and faster route, the Soviet Union's State Defense Committee decided in October, 1941, to begin the necessary preparatory work.[16]

V. Molokov, chief of Aeroflot,[17] was given the responsibility for making the ALSIB survey. He organized a team of specialists that included prominent flyers with polar and Siberian aviation experience. After considering various possible trans-Siberian avenues, the team recommended the east-to-west route from Uel'kal through Seymchan, Yakutsk, and Kirensk to Krasnoyarsk.

The 3,500-mile route was over one of Siberia's vast virgin stretches of tundra, mountains, and forests. Roads that pilots customarily used for familiar reference points did not exist, nor did navigation aids. While the selected route was far from ideal, it did have certain advantages. The only over-water flying was the short distance from Alaska across the Bering Sea to Uel'kal. Certain sections of the route were already familiar to pioneer polar and Aeroflot pilots. The weather, although severe in winter, was generally stable along most of the route. Because Krasnoyarsk, located on the Trans-Siberian Railroad, was the route termination, the arriving aircraft could be moved closer to the war front by rail if necessary. And finally, the route fulfilled the requirement of being located far enough to the north for its operation not to be a major irritant to Japan.

The survey having been completed, the State Defense Committee promptly approved the ALSIB route project. As soon as weather permitted in early 1942, resources were mobilized to transport construction materials, to assign flying, engineering, and service personnel, to stockpile fuel and lubricants, and to establish weather, communication, and other vital services for the five key bases. By Soviet standards, the completion of an aviation project on the scale of the ALSIB route was estimated to require four to five years, yet only ten months after the State Defense Committee made its initial decision, the somewhat primitive route was declared ready to begin the ferrying operation.[18]

The air bases in the beginning (1942) depended almost entirely on supplies delivered by air transport, a situation that quickly became a logistical nightmare. In 1943, matters eased somewhat when cargo vessels for the first time entered the Arctic Ocean via the Bering Strait during

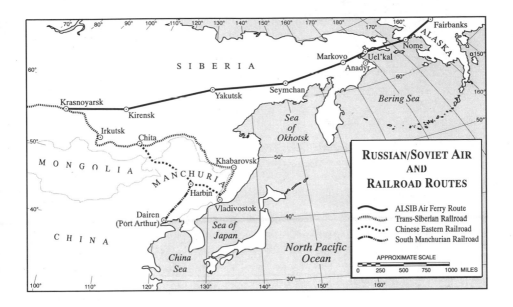

the four summer months, June–September. The supply ships reached the mouths of the south-to-north flowing Kolyma, Lena, and Yenisei rivers, on which the vital cargoes were further transported upstream to Seymchan, Yakutsk, and even Krasnoyarsk. During the summers of 1943, 1944, and 1945, a total of a half million tons of essential Lend-Lease supplies was delivered to the air bases.[19]

The conception of the ALSIB route in the Soviet Union was an accepted fact, but the final labor pains leading to its birth were still to come.

In the midst of mobilizing American resources and industries to support Lend-Lease promises, the United States herself was abruptly at war with Axis foes. Churchill rushed to Washington to confer with Roosevelt. In their Arcadia Conference at Christmastime in 1941, they agreed on a war policy that also would guide their future relationship with Stalin. Defeat of Germany was the primary objective. Defeat of Japan would come later. While the Red Army engaged the German forces in the Soviet Union, the Western Allies pledged a "second front" in Europe. Launching the second front, however, depended on extensive planning and preparation. Therefore, the flow of Lend-Lease aid to the Red Army must not only be maintained but must increase. In the absence of a prompt second front, the fulfillment of America's Lend-Lease agreements would continue to be used to glue the Soviet-American alliance together.[20]

Once the United States was at war, pressure mounted in Washington for ways to get American base rights in Siberia. By March, 1942, Stalin was more suspicious than ever of any U.S. move that he believed might involve the Soviet Union in war with Japan. In addition, Stalin was especially upset by the trickle rather the full flow of Lend-Lease assistance that had been promised. Unfortunately, shipments to the Soviet Union fell behind for sundry reasons, such as the steady ship losses on the North route and the disorganization and slow deliveries on the South route.

American military officials, unaware of the Soviet Union's progressing preparations, renewed their interest in use of the ALSIB route. Moreover, their idea that American pilots could ferry Lend-Lease airplanes to Siberian bases for transfer to the Soviets was still alive. And to pave the way for American entrée in Siberia, they realized that agreement must be reached with Stalin to bring the ALSIB route to life.[21] Hence in April, 1942, during his first meeting in Moscow with Stalin, William Standley, the new U.S. ambassador, again broached the subject of the ALSIB ferry route. Stalin said that Japan might object. He promised, however, to think about it.[22]

Meanwhile, Stalin decided to send Foreign Minister V. M. Molotov to London and Washington to discuss the second front that Stalin expected to relieve the pressure on the Red Army.[23] Molotov arrived to meet and talk with Roosevelt on May 30. During the subsequent discussions, Molotov received a copy of the draft Second Protocol covering Lend-Lease commitments for the forthcoming period of July, 1942, through June, 1943.[24] When questioned about the status of an ALSIB route, Molotov said that he did not know what decision was being reached in Moscow.[25]

However, a few days later on June 8, Maxime Litvinov, the new Soviet ambassador to the U.S., met with Harry Hopkins and announced that the Soviet government was agreeable to the operation of the ALSIB route.[26]

At the time of the Hopkins-Litvinov conversation, Japanese landing forces successfully occupied the westernmost Aleutian Islands of Kiska and Attu. The occupation immediately called attention to what may have been a prelude to Japanese military movement toward Siberia. On June 17, Roosevelt wrote to Stalin and expressed both his pleasure with the Soviets' positive decision regarding the ALSIB route and his concern for the new danger of a Japanese attack in the Soviet Far East.

On June 23, Roosevelt wrote a follow-up letter to Stalin, advising him that "I am prepared to instruct the American ferry crews to deliver aircraft to you at Lake Baikal [Siberia]. . . . [In the event of a Japanese attack on the Soviet Maritime Provinces] this air route could be easily connected up with landing fields leading into the Vladivostok area . . .

[and] would permit the United States quickly [to come to] the assistance of the Soviet Union."[27]

A week later, Stalin personally confirmed the agreement to open the ALSIB route, but at the same time he again quashed the American notion of gaining access to Siberian bases. He wrote that he shared Roosevelt's opinion that time could be saved in transferring aircraft to the war front via Alaska and Siberia. "Taking this into consideration," he said, "the Soviet Government has already given the necessary instructions to complete all operations in Siberia in preparation for the reception of planes in the shortest possible time. . . . As to whose pilots should fly the planes from Alaska, it seems to me that can be assigned to . . . Soviet airmen."[28]

Once having decided to make the ALSIB route operational, Stalin became impatient. On July 2, he met with Ambassador Standley and belittled any suggestion of further discussions between Soviet and American officials in Washington. He told Standley that "already [there is] too much talk. Our fields are ready to receive planes. All I want to know is how many per month and when."[29]

Stalin agreed to receive a U.S. representative in Moscow to develop the details of the ALSIB route operation. He likewise agreed to an American suggestion that a team be named to survey the condition of the Siberian air bases. Stalin made it clear, however, that the work of the representative and the survey team was to further only one objective— to initiate the aircraft ferry operation over the ALSIB route.[30]

The timing of the route's final prenatal activity came when Soviet-American relations were reaching a new low point. The unfulfilled promises of a second front, the suspension of Allied convoys on the North route, the poor delivery performance on the South route, and the fierce German drive toward Stalingrad and the oil-rich Caucasus all came into focus in the summer of 1942. The suspicious Soviets made no secret of their bitterness as Lend-Lease shipments continued to fall behind schedule.[31]

On July 4, Ambassador Standley informed Roosevelt that Stalin was ready to activate the ALSIB route. Army Air Force Maj. Gen. Follett Bradley was selected to be the U.S. representative in the crucial Moscow negotiations.

To prepare for his visit to Moscow, Bradley conferred on July 18 with Maj. Gen. Alexander Belyaev, chairman of the Soviet Purchasing Commission in Washington and the Soviet official through whom Lend-Lease matters were coordinated. To Belyaev, Bradley countered the Soviet assumption that only Soviets would make the Siberian route survey. Bradley requested that an American team be included in a joint Soviet-American survey group. Surprisingly, the Soviets did not quibble. Stalin responded that Soviet planes bearing the Soviet survey team would arrive at Fairbanks on August 10 to pick up the American surveyors and then wait for Soviet clearance to proceed. When the Soviet-American group finally was cleared to depart from Fairbanks to Siberia in late August, the group included seven Americans commanded by Col. Alva Harvey.[32]

Meanwhile, Bradley and his crew in the latest model B-24 heavy bomber made a ten-day flight from Washington south to Brazil, across the Atlantic Ocean and Africa, north to Cairo, east to Tehran and then to Moscow, arriving on August 6.[33]

General Bradley immediately initiated the first of a series of meetings during the following weeks with General Sterligov, the Soviet representative for the conduct of the delicate negotiations. Army Air Force planners still hoped that the U.S. offer to ferry Lend-Lease aircraft to Siberian airfields would be acceptable. However, if the Soviets continued to reject the idea, the alternative point of transfer in Alaska was either Nome or Fairbanks. When Col. George Brewer had previously looked at available bases in Alaska, he had recommended Fairbanks over Nome because of better facilities and better weather conditions. After Bradley again raised the subject of Siberian versus Alaskan point of transfer, the Soviet reaction was so rigid that Bradley was quickly convinced that any further discussion was futile. Fairbanks, Alaska, he told Sterligov, was acceptable.[34]

In Washington, General Belyaev was advised that sixty-six Lend-Lease bombers were scheduled to arrive in Alaska for transfer within ten days after the ALSIB route's final approval, with nearly a hundred fighters soon to follow.[35] Faced with the prospect of such delivery volume, the Soviets asked for forty-three C-47 transport aircraft to operate the route in Siberia.[36] Since C-47 transports were in critical short supply, the War Department refused the Soviet request for forty-three but offered to provide ten.

In Moscow, Bradley was concerned that the Soviets might use the refusal as an excuse to abandon activation of the ferry route. He assured his Soviet counterpart, General Sterligov, that the United States was willing to undertake operation of the entire ALSIB route if necessary. After Soviets and Americans sparred in both Washington and Moscow, the Soviets ignored Bradley's offer and decided to accept the ten transports.[37]

The crisis over, the transport issue seemed to fade. The Soviet-American joint survey group waiting in Fairbanks, having now been cleared by the Kremlin to begin the ALSIB route inspection, entered Siberia. Bradley himself planned to meet Colonel Harvey and the joint group at Krasnoyarsk and then accompany them to Moscow, but the route survey was completed before Bradley obtained official Soviet permission to travel. On his arrival at Moscow, Harvey reported to Bradley that most of the bases between the Bering Sea and Krasnoyarsk were primitive but those between Krasnoyarsk and Moscow were modern by comparison. Harvey said, however, that if the primitive bases were adequately supplied, Lend-Lease aircraft could be successfully flown from point to point.[38]

While Harvey viewed the condition of the proposed ALSIB route in a favorable light, the Soviets reacted with caution. When American planners in Washington advised General Belyaev that the latest Lend-Lease delivery projection called for 415 planes to be sent over the ALSIB route in September and October, Belyaev said that the route would not be able to handle that volume. A revised plan lowered the number of aircraft to 142 per month until such time as route capacity improved.[39]

On September 1, 1942, as a result of Colonel Harvey's favorable report, General Bradley, acting on behalf of the U.S. government, advised General Sterligov of the American approval of the ALSIB route. Taking Bradley's announcement as final, the Soviets refused to allow Harvey to make a more detailed inspection as originally planned, claiming that it was no longer necessary.[40] A Soviet transport returned Harvey and his survey team directly from Moscow to Alaska.

In early August, 1942, Col. Ilya P. Mazuruk was commander of the Red Air Force's 2nd Air Group composed of polar aviation airmen operating in the Barents, White, and Kara seas area. Without any warning, Mazuruk was ordered to report to Moscow immediately. Upon arrival, he found that the ALSIB route was being scheduled for operational use as soon as possible. Since Stalin had insisted that Lend-Lease aircraft would be ferried from Fairbanks across Siberia only by Soviet airmen, Mazuruk had been chosen to organize and direct the ALSIB route's activities.[41]

Despite Stalin's earlier claim that the ferry route was ready for use, it was not. Time was short. Three of the Siberian air bases—Uel'kal, Seymchan, and Kirensk—were in a questionable state of preparedness after having been carved from the wilderness. A hastily created organization to conduct the ferrying operations was still evolving. To serve the route, Mazuruk was given command of the unique new 1st Ferrying Aviation Division, comprising five regiments, one for each of the five "regions" through which thousands of Lend-Lease aircraft would later pass.

The 1st Ferrying Aviation Regiment was assigned to the primary region, extending from Fairbanks and Nome across the Bering Sea to Uel'kal. Alternate emergency landing fields were at Galena and later at Moses

Point, both in western Alaska. The 2nd Ferrying Aviation Regiment served the next region, from Uel'kal to Seymchan, with an alternate landing field at Markovo for refueling when necessary. An emergency landing strip was also available at Anadyr but could be used only in winter when the ground was frozen. Serving the interior Siberian region from Seymchan to Yakutsk was the 3rd Ferrying Aviation Regiment, while the 4th forwarded aircraft across the next interior region from Yakutsk to Kirensk. And the 5th Ferrying Aviation Regiment was responsible for delivering the Lend-Lease planes to the ALSIB route's terminal base at Krasnoyarsk.

According to Colonel Mazuruk's operating plans,[42] an attached auxiliary unit, the 8th Ferrying Aviation Regiment, was required to function exclusively as a transport organization with five transport squadrons, one for each region. Bomber and fighter ferry pilots from one regiment would pass their Lend-Lease aircraft to the pilots of the next regiment until all of the ALSIB route's five regions had been traversed. When ferry pilots landed their planes at the designated relay base, the airmen were returned via transport to their home bases for rest and assignment to another delivery mission. By this shuttle process, ferry pilots gained familiarity and confidence that was reflected in the ALSIB route's steadily improved performance.

In late August, the pilots and crews needed to open the ALSIB route were hastily being identified and assembled for assignment to the cadres of the ferrying regiments. Men destined to pioneer the ALSIB primarily were from two military sources: recently hospitalized airmen who were recuperating from battle injuries, and experienced aviators transferred from the South route ferrying operation in Iraq and Iran. Other airmen who were being given respite from the fierce air battles at the front soon followed. Lt. Col. Nikifor Vasin's exhausted 185th Fighter Aviation Regiment in its entirety was disengaged from combat, reformed, and distributed among the ALSIB route's ferrying units. As a result of having rammed a German plane in combat, Vasin himself had lost front teeth and his flashing steel replacements were visible badges of honor. He later became the permanent commander of the 1st Ferrying Aviation Regiment based at Fairbanks.[43]

In addition, an Aeroflot transport regiment was assigned to the ferry route. Many of these airmen had been battle-tested evacuating trapped civilians from combat zones and delivering supplies to partisan groups behind German lines. Some of the Aeroflot personnel were sent to the 8th Regiment's transport squadrons, and others were selected for retraining as fighter ferry pilots. A modified YAK-7 fighter with special dual controls was used for the transition training, first at Krasnoyarsk and later at Yakutsk. Victor Perov, who became a well-known fighter ferry pilot, was in charge of the retraining program.[44] The Aeroflot auxiliaries were integrated into the Red Air Force for the duration of the war.

Before World War II, the Canadian government had been intrigued by the dream of a future great circle aviation route to the Orient and had encouraged the development of commercial airfields in western Canada. As war approached in 1941, Canadian and U.S. joint military planners foresaw the need for an improved commercial aviation route to Alaska. The Canadian government, using Canadian funds and Canadian contractors, began to expand the existing airfields and build additional landing strips from Edmonton to Alaska. The new development became the Northwest Staging Route,[45] also later referred to as the Northwest air route or simply the Northwest route.

Once at war with Japan, the Canadian and U.S. governments quickly reached agreement in March, 1942, to build 1,500 miles of gravel road through the rugged Canadian Rocky Mountains.[46] The gigantic construction project that became the Alaska Highway was planned to provide an emergency land connection to Alaska and a ground supply linkage to the current and future Northwest route airfields.[47]

The U.S. Army was given the responsibility. In an incredible achievement, U.S. Army engineer regiments and American and Canadian civilian contractors forged an unimproved road from Dawson Creek, British Columbia, to Big Delta, Alaska, in nine months. At Big Delta, the new roadway connected with the existing highway to Fairbanks, where an official highway opening ceremony was held on November 20, 1942. Necessary improvements continued to be made during 1943 to make the highway usable.[48] The Alaska Highway never became an emergency land supply artery to Alaska because Japan never disrupted the sea supply line to Alaska.[49] However, the highway did provide essential service to the Northwest route during the height of Lend-Lease aircraft ferrying operations across Canada to Fairbanks in 1943–45.[50]

In contrast to the rapid development of the road, air base construction on the Northwest route was behind schedule in early 1942. Nonetheless, the pioneer air route began to be tested by aircraft being ferried to the Eleventh Air Force in Alaska. Plans were made to carry priority military cargo to Alaska and, to reinforce the route's transport service, contracts were made with American civilian airlines.[51]

The birth of the ALSIB route was near. Now that Fairbanks had been designated as the point where Lend-Lease aircraft would be delivered to

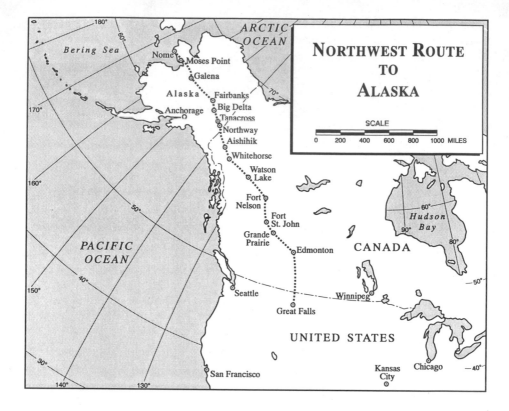

Soviet control, the Americans faced the task of organizing and operating the Northwest route between Great Falls, Montana (Gore Field), and Fairbanks (Ladd Field).

On June 20, 1942, while Soviet-American expectations regarding the ALSIB route were rising and Japanese landing forces were occupying the outer Aleutian Islands, the Army Air Force established the new Air Transport Command (ATC). Responsibility for operating the Northwest route was given immediately to ATC's Ferrying Division.

Sensing the urgency of the current situation, elements of the 7th Ferrying Group were already en route from their home base in Seattle to Great Falls when the formal movement orders were received on June 22. Four days later, on June 26, Col. William Tunner of the ATC's Ferrying Division gave Lt. Col. Leroy P. de Arce, commander of the 7th Ferrying Group, his mission: "You will take necessary action to organize and operate a ferrying route between Great Falls, Montana and Fairbanks, Alaska, through Lethbridge, Calgary, Edmonton, Fort St. John, Fort Nelson, Watson Lake and Whitehorse, Canada and through Northway and Big Delta, Alaska."[52]

The statement of mission was simple and short but its execution was not. Following Stalin's literal blessing of the ALSIB route and the War Department's plan to send General Bradley to Moscow, the 7th Ferrying Group swiftly came under pressure: the Northwest route must be opened to Lend-Lease aircraft traffic in the shortest possible time. Crucial decisions were made. By mid-July, men and supplies were filtered to stations on the route, and by mid-August an approved ferrying organization emerged.

Colonel de Arce was confirmed as the Northwest route commander. He was responsible for the route's operation and supply as well as the actual delivery of Lend-Lease aircraft to Fairbanks. He divided his command into three sectors, each managed by an air base headquarters squadron and each containing a number of route stations. One squadron was responsible for the southern sector from Great Falls to Edmonton, another for the Canadian sector from Edmonton to Whitehorse, and the third for the Alaskan sector. The squadron commanders were in charge of all functions involving the ferrying of aircraft through their respective territories.[53]

On August 26, Maj. Raymond F. Kitchingman, together with a small advance party from his base squadron, landed at Ladd Field to assume responsibilities for the ATC Alaskan sector. In addition to Ladd Field, Kitchingman's other designated Alaskan operational bases included Northway, Tanacross, Big Delta, Galena, and Nome.[54] Located near the southeastern edge of Fairbanks, Ladd Field was regarded as the most comfortable and best equipped military installation in Alaska, with heated pedestrian tunnels linking the buildings and with Hangar One as its most visible landmark. The Soviets who later flew to and from the Fairbanks base called it a "rest camp."

The first authorized major air base in Alaska, Ladd Field was originally built to be the home of the Cold Weather Experimental Station, the first commander of which was Maj. Dale Gaffney. Later, the organization's name was changed to the Cold Weather Test Detachment (CWTD). In June, 1942, when the Japanese landings in the Aleutians produced a military alert throughout Alaska, the CWTD was temporarily disbanded and its personnel and aircraft dispersed for the defense of the state. Most of the CWTD's men were merged with troops massed at Nome on June 22. Later, when the immediate threat to Nome faded, the CWTD was formally reestablished and its men and planes were scheduled to return to Ladd Field in October.[55]

The Alaskan air stations selected for the ATC ferrying operation were under the control of the Eleventh Air Force, the air arm of the Alaska Defense Command (ADC). Because the Eleventh Air Force's attention was directed to the Japanese thrust into the Aleutians, the neglected air stations at Northway, Tanacross, Big Delta, and Galena were ill prepared for the new ferrying mission. Ladd Field was in better shape, as was Nome because of the recent concentration of army and air forces there. However, the Nome garrison, commanded by Brig. Gen. Edwin W. Jones, and the adjacent Eleventh Air Force base, newly designated as Marks Field, were still considered essential to the Bering Sea defenses. Ladd Field's facilities, although well organized, were not ready to meet the expanded requirements of the abruptly imposed ATC mission. Ladd Field was already burdened with numerous combat, administrative, and service support units as well as the 6th Air Depot Group, the Alaska Air Depot, and the Ladd Field Sub-Depot.[56]

On August 27, General Buckner acted quickly. Using his authority as head of the Alaska Defense Command, he ordered the commanding general of the Eleventh Air Force, the commanding general at Nome, and the commanding officer at Ladd Field to plan for and give necessary support to the ATC's ferrying operations. The open-ended order remained in effect until ATC was able to assume responsibility for the bases at some future date. In the meantime, ATC's status at the Alaskan stations was that of a tenant.[57]

When Major Kitchingman arrived at Ladd Field on August 26, he carried with him a terse eight-point memorandum of instructions from the commanding general of the ATC Ferrying Division:

1. You are responsible that quarters and messing are available for U.S. and Russian crews. You will make all necessary arrangements with representatives of the commanding officer, Ladd Field.
2. You will, when the flow of aircraft becomes regular, regulate the flow by advising [Colonel] de Arce at Great Falls.
3. You will be responsible for transition training but not more than transition training; if more is required, you will advise at once.
4. You will be responsible for loading and unloading of cargo planes.
5. You will be responsible for operation, maintenance and condition of outlying fields which are assigned to our jurisdiction. You will be responsible for assignment of men to these fields.
6. You will be responsible that all cargo aircraft are properly cleared.
7. You will be responsible for the transfer of land-based planes to the Russians.
8. You will clear all Russian planes into proper weather. You will instruct Russians as to our codes so that they may proceed across and out of Alaska.[58]

The ATC responsibilities in Alaska were complex, and coping with them effectively would require additional organization, logistical support, and manpower. But before members of Kitchingman's advance party could catch their breath, they were faced with their first crisis:

The Soviets were coming!

Often without warning and not always welcome, other Soviet-American crises occurred at later times at Ladd Field and Nome. This first crisis, however, actually brought a sense of relief and was therefore welcome. Because, even though the ATC organization was unprepared and undermanned for volume ferry traffic, the coming of the Soviets was considered to be a signal that the birth of the ALSIB route was truly imminent.

Unfortunately, the signal was premature. Another delay, an almost fatal one, remained to be overcome.

4.
ALSIB
Route at Last!

Despite disruptive diplomatic cross-signals, the Fairbanks Lend-Lease transfer point and the ALSIB route connection underwent initial testing in September and October, 1942. The first deliveries arrived, but instead of the expected rate of 142 aircraft per month, the numbers were disappointingly small for a variety of reasons. Spare parts shortages and winter modification problems were contributing factors. Weather conditions and navigational hazards in Canada and Alaska were handicaps, and the hastily assembled ATC ferrying organization lacked sufficient time to to plan, equip, and operate an effective Lend-Lease aircraft delivery system.[1]

Within hours of the arrival of ATC's advance party on August 26, 1942, the first resident Soviets landed at Ladd Field from Washington, D.C.: Serge A. Piskounov and Alexis A. Anisimov. These two officials represented the Soviet Purchasing Commission while waiting for additional staff members to join them. Anisimov later replaced Piskounov as the senior Soviet civilian in Alaska. Earlier in August, Col. Alva Harvey's American team members had joined a Soviet team to begin the survey of the proposed ferry route across Siberia. But the Soviet team members had only been visitors at Ladd Field. Piskounov and Anisimov were not visitors. They arrived to establish what seemed to be a committed Soviet presence in Alaska.[2]

This Lend-Lease bomber is ready to fly "Texaco"! Capt. Roman P. Pokrovsky, an engineer at Ladd Field, inspects the temporary Soviet aircraft insignia made with a local Texaco service station star decal. Courtesy George Kisevalter

Behind the scenes, Major Kitchingman was involved in the early process of marrying the ATC Northwest route to the Soviets' promised ALSIB route, and other American and Soviet historic actions were soon under way.

On September 3, ATC ferry pilots brought the first Lend-Lease aircraft—five A-20 light bombers—to Ladd Field after a two-day flight from Great Falls.[3] These aircraft bore the white star insignia of the U.S. armed forces. After each plane was officially transferred to the Soviets and prepared for its long, pioneering flight over the ALSIB route, a similar star insignia adorned the fuselage and wings—but now the white star was red. Later, when Lend-Lease processing procedures were better organized at Great Falls, the red star insignia of the Red Air Force was automatically painted on each of the thousands of Lend-Lease airplanes en route to Fairbanks.

Also on September 3, two battered Soviet Li-2 transports from Siberia landed at Nome, carrying key personnel to organize the Soviet Military Mission and reinforce the Soviet Purchasing Commission staff in Alaska. After remaining overnight at Nome, the transports flew to their final destination at Fairbanks the next day. Among the twenty-six passengers were Col. Michael G. Machin, commanding officer of the military mission; Col. Peter S. Kiselev, chief of the mission's technical and inspection services; NKVD Lt. Makary F. Komar, who later became involved in an international crisis at Ladd Field (chap. 6); and Lt. Elena A. Makarova and Lt. Natasha Fenelonova, both fluent linguists who converted critical technical data from English into Russian. As key technical interpreters, they were essential staff officers in the military mission.[4]

Makarova and Fenelonova were graduates of the Military Faculty of the Institute of Foreign Languages and held the rank of lieutenant in the Red Army's administrative service. When the Lend-Lease South route was first established, the women had been sent to Tehran, Iran, to serve as interpreters.[5] "Soviet pilots ferried the Lend-Lease bombers from Basra, Iraq through Tehran to Moscow," Makarova recalled. "At Tehran where Natasha and I were stationed, a group of Soviet military engineers inspected each of the planes for technical acceptance before delivery to Moscow."

She admitted that "none of our engineers knew very much about the new American airplanes, so we, engineers and interpreters, learned together. From being technically ignorant about the airplanes in the beginning, Natasha and I progressed to the point of being able, based on our experience of translating and interpreting technical data for the engineers, to become technicians in our own right."

While at Tehran, Makarova met Lt. Peter Gamov, one of the ferry pilots who frequently flew Lend-Lease bombers to Moscow. "Peter would deliver our small gift parcels to our friends and relatives," she said. Being army officers, the two women wore military uniforms. "They were uncomfortable and inconvenient for various reasons," she remembered. "In August [1942] when we were selected to leave Iran and go to Alaska, we suggested to our senior officers that we dress as civilians, not officers, when we went there. They agreed."

In addition to Makarova and Fenelonova, many of the Soviet engineers who had been in Tehran were also sent to Alaska. The entire group of twenty-six was assembled and already en route across Siberia even before General Bradley in Moscow was informing Washington on September 1 that the Soviet government had finally approved the use of the ALSIB route.[6] According to Makarova, the Soviet group was divided

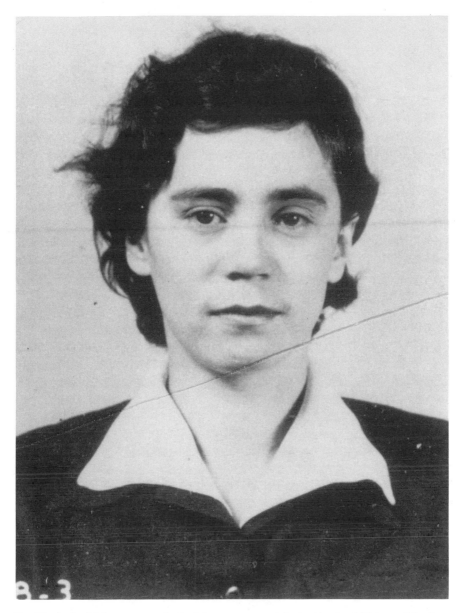

Lt. Elena A. Makarova, technical interpreter with the Soviet Military Mission at Fairbanks, 1942–44. She later married Capt. Peter Gamov, 1st Ferrying Aviation Regiment. Courtesy George Kisevalter

Lt. Natasha Fenelonova, technical interpreter with the Soviet Military Mission, 1942–45. She and Sr. Sgt. Nicholas Tiurin were married at Fairbanks in early 1945. Courtesy Elena Makarova

between the two transports in order to avoid the possible loss of the entire group if one of the planes should crash.

"When we arrived at Nome, all of the Americans who met us at the air base were surprised to see two girls among the men," Makarova related. "Because we were not married to any of the men, the Americans said that there was no suitable place for us at the air base and, in spite of Colonel Machin's protests, they sent us to the only hotel in Nome. The hotel's owner was a very respectable woman who supposed that we were *waitresses*! We tried to explain that we were *interpreters*, but she did not understand."

The two women had a bath "which we long needed" and went to bed. Soon there was a knock at the door. "It was our hotel hostess," Makarova continued. "She told us that the Nome garrison officers had organized a banquet in our honor, and for the occasion they had decorated the banquet table with all the flowers to be found in Nome."

Makarova and Fenelonova did not know what to do. Their travel clothing was half military and half civilian, but was this the proper attire for their first formal meeting with Americans? Was it proper in America for two girls without escorts to be alone among the men?

"We did not have answers," Makarova said, "so we excused ourselves by saying that we were very, very tired. We decided that we would have to be very careful in the future so that we could retain the respect due to Soviet girls and that we should never violate any American customs."

After the Soviet group arrived at Ladd Field the next day, Makarova reported that "we were horrified by another incident. On our way to our assigned office, Natasha and I had to pass through the large hangar [Hangar One]. It seemed quite empty except for several planes standing at the far end. When we passed them, we suddenly heard a loud whistle. My God!" Makarova exclaimed, "what were the Americans taking us for? First, we were waitresses in Nome, and now what? . . . In the Soviet Union, men whistled at girls whom they considered to be not quite decent, to say the least!

"There were so many things to be learned about American customs. We later found out that when American men whistled at you, they did not mean dishonor. We also discovered that all the Americans who knew us had a high opinion of us."[7]

With the new arrivals, Ladd Field had twenty-eight resident Soviets. Installed in an officers' quarters and a barracks, they began to develop an operating procedure for the anticipated transfer of Lend-Lease aircraft.

"Natasha and I were the only technical interpreters at Ladd Field,"

Makarova said. "There were Russian-speaking Americans on the base, but still Colonel Machin and Colonel Kiselev preferred our help."

Later, when the ALSIB route became fully operational, the Soviet pilots rested when the weather did not permit flying. "There was no rest for us, however," Makarova said. "There was so much written aircraft technical material to be translated. When we were not otherwise occupied, translation was an everyday occupation for us."

Shortly after delivering the Soviet cadres to Ladd Field, the two Li-2 transports were reloaded with Lend-Lease freight and disappeared from Alaska across the Bering Sea.[8] At this time, the only Soviet communication between Ladd Field and the Soviet bases in Siberia was the hourly contact for exchange of weather information. Unable to issue direct orders regarding the movement of the first group of ferrying crews from Siberia to Alaska, the Soviet Military Mission at Ladd Field relied on uncensored administrative messages sent to Siberia via Washington and Moscow. On September 20, however, ATC learned that direct communication between Fairbanks or Nome and Siberian bases was authorized for the Soviets to exchange operational information. The Soviets were permitted to transmit messages in code, but only if the messages were decipherable by ATC.[9]

Despite the early communications problem involving Soviet aircraft movement of ferrying crews across Siberia, the Soviet Military Mission expected the group of ferrying crews to reach Ladd Field in the near future, weather permitting. In the meantime, 7th Ferrying Group pilots delivered thirty P-40 fighters, six C-47 transports, and nine additional A-20 light bombers to Ladd Field.[10]

While Makarova and Fenelonova adjusted to life at Fairbanks, the fate of the ALSIB route apparently still hung in the balance. With personnel poised in the final stages of ferry route preparation at numerous points in Alaska and Siberia, General Bradley tried to extend his dialogue with Kremlin officials to probe the likelihood of Soviet-American joint planning if a Soviet-Japanese war should occur. These efforts did not produce any tangible results. While waiting for the outcome of his inquiries, however, Bradley accompanied U.S. Ambassador Standley to visit five American flyers interned in the Ural Mountains.[11] (The internees were crew members on one of the bombers led by Lt. Col. James H. Doolittle in his famous raid on Tokyo in April. Short on fuel, the five flyers landed safely in Soviet Far East.)

Then, to Bradley's astonishment, a new round of uncertainty afflicted the ALSIB route. On September 19, General Belyaev in Washington unexpectedly announced that the Soviet government had decided that the route was not suitable for use! The classic question of whether the ALSIB route was to be or not to be was back on the table. Clear reasons for Belyaev's announcement never emerged. This setback, however, was sufficient for the exasperated War Department to flash a red light, stopping the movement of designated Lend-Lease aircraft bound for Alaska.

For two weeks, confusion and crossed communication prevailed. Then the War Department advised Bradley in Moscow on October 4 that the U.S. government would no longer consider the ALSIB route for Lend-Lease delivery. On the same day, Bradley notified Washington that the Soviet government had had a change of mind. The Soviets, Bradley announced, intended to open the ALSIB route as planned for continuous future use. In view of Bradley's welcome message, the War Department reconsidered its decision. The Soviet-American resolution came in time to resuscitate the almost stillborn ALSIB route.[12]

On September 24, during the first week of unexplained Soviet vacillation that endangered the activation of the route, five Soviet transport planes accompanied by a B-25 bomber arrived at Ladd Field. The arriving aircraft brought ferrying crews for eighteen bombers, forty fighters, and seven transports. They had originally been scheduled to reach Alaska a week earlier, but weather conditions had grounded them at Uel'kal.[13] Among the pilots were Lt. Col. Pavel Nedosekin, the designated acting commander of the fledgling 1st Ferrying Aviation Regiment, and Lt. Peter P. Gamov, Elena Makarova's friend from the South route in Iran.

Although the War Department had frozen further Lend-Lease deliveries, fifty airplanes were waiting at the Fairbanks transfer point when the Soviet ferrying crews arrived. The War Department authorized the release of forty-four aircraft (A-20s and P-40s) but ordered the return of six (C-47s) to Great Falls.[14]

Transition training for the bomber and fighter pilots began immediately. Five ATC officers from Kitchingman's advance party were assigned to acquaint the pilots with the operational characteristics of the American aircraft. Only one of the American officers spoke Russian, but both Soviets and Americans became skillful in using improvised sign language. Since the Soviet pilots were reported to be experienced flyers, their transition training was limited to cockpit and instrument familiarization as well as takeoff, flight, and landing practice, including the use of air base traffic control procedures.[15]

On September 29, five days after their arrival at Ladd Field, the Soviet pilots were eager to ferry a flight of twelve A-20 bombers to Nome en route to Siberia. Colonel Nedosekin was the leader of the group, and

Capt. Louis Klam (*left*) of ATC and Capt. Peter P. Gamov, daring Soviet bomber ferry pilot between Fairbanks and Uel'kal, Siberia, photographed at Nome in 1944. Courtesy Army Air Force

Lieutenant Gamov was one of his pilots. The historic flight marked the start of Gamov's colorful and lengthy career as the future commander of the 1st Bomber Squadron in the Ladd Field-based ferrying regiment. The weather was favorable, and all twelve bombers reached Nome without any mishap. However, the bombers were grounded on arrival after persistent engine piston ring problems were discovered. Rush-ordered replacement rings were delivered by air and installed at Nome.

Also on September 29, four of the Soviet transports that had brought the ferrying pilots to Ladd Field departed for Nome and onward to Siberia. The transports were laden with a portion of the fifteen tons of Lend-Lease spare parts and field equipment for Soviet use along the ALSIB route.

On October 6, a week after being grounded at Nome, ten of the A-20 bombers continued their flight to Siberia. One had to return to Nome because of a malfunction, and another made a forced landing on Siberian soil. The remaining eight flew three hundred miles beyond Uel'kal to Markovo.[16] Continuing from Markovo, the eight bombers traversed the untested ALSIB route, encountering numerous unanticipated delays and finally reaching Krasnoyarsk on November 11, five weeks after leaving Nome. It was not an inspiring operational beginning for the ALSIB route, but considering the many problems in bringing the route to life, it was an international achievement of note. The official ALSIB connection was now a fact; the first fitful steps in its operational life of three years had been accomplished. Given time and cooperation, the route would develop the capability of ferrying thousands of combat aircraft to the war front in a matter of days, not weeks or months.

Except for three P-40 fighters, the remainder of the original forty-four fighters and bombers released to the Soviets were flown from Fairbanks to Nome, beginning on October 9. From Nome, they departed in several separate flights between October 10 and 15. One P-40 fighter was forced to return to Alaska because of an engine fire over the Bering Sea. The Soviet pilot managed to reach land, where the fighter crashed and burned a few miles from Nome. The pilot survived.[17]

The daring Soviet pilots of these early Lend-Lease airplanes were the unheralded trailblazers for other pilots to follow. The conditions that they found at the various stations in 1942 were harsh, and conditions worsened as the Siberian winter approached. In lieu of shelter and adequate equipment, the ground crews devised hasty innovations to ensure that the aircraft shuttle from station to station was maintained, weather permitting. After the first winter passed, more personnel and construction brought improvements to handle the flow of aircraft over the route.[18]

The first destination for the Siberian-bound airplanes was usually Uel'kal. In 1942, Uel'kal's primitive airfield consisted of a runway and a taxi strip located on a spit of land near Kresta Bay. Although a few buildings were nearby, neither hangars nor barracks were available. The runway itself was built on a framework of wooden poles laid side by side in corduroy fashion. In winter, the gaps between the poles were filled with sand and clay that made a smooth frozen surface for landings and takeoffs. During the spring thaw in 1943, ships delivered metal sheets to cover the runway for summer use.

Ground crews and airmen were generally housed in circular huts some twenty feet in diameter and covered with skins or sod, usually the latter. Inside, each hut was partitioned, pie-cut style, into ten sleeping stalls and was heated by a lone central stove.

Aircraft being ferried over the route were deliberately slowed to less than two hundred miles per hour in order to conserve fuel. Pilots therefore were aloft for several hours while traversing their assigned legs of the route. The adjustment to longer hours in the air was especially difficult for the veteran fighter pilots accustomed to flying short combat sorties. Moreover, the extra fuel tanks suspended from the fighters' wings tested the pilots' ability to control their craft, particularly in bad weather.

Because the airplanes were usually flown at high altitudes—between seventeen and twenty-two thousand feet—in very low temperatures, the pilots wore oxygen masks in unheated cockpits. Pilots were further hampered by frosted cockpit windows that limited visibility. Portions of the route were flown by instrument when forest fire smoke in summer and heavy fog and clouds in winter obscured terrain features.[19]

Like the Soviets on the ALSIB route, the American pilots on the Northwest route in October of 1942 were operating literally on the proverbial wing and prayer. In many respects, the Northwest route mirrored the trials of the route in Siberia. It crossed vast expanses of rugged mountains and forestlands with few recognizable landmarks. In winter, temperatures dipped to lows comparable to those in Siberia. At the start, few dependable radio navigational aids were available. The lives of the ferry pilots were jeopardized when radio signals became distorted by the northern lights and like disturbances peculiar to the subarctic region. The Northwest route, however, had one advantage: distances between available landing fields did not exceed three hundred miles. In Siberia, the ALSIB route pilots flew as far as eight hundred miles to reach the next landing field.

Grim as were the early conditions on both routes, the Soviet and American attitudes were positive. Both groups realized that their respective operations were being thrust into a cruel and hazardous environment. They also knew that man-made improvements in the operating conditions on the routes were absolutely essential. Soviets and Americans alike faced the challenge of their first winter, now approaching.

During the September 19–October 4 hiatus in establishment of the ALSIB route, the flow of designated Lend-Lease planes to Alaska had been stopped and then reversed. In an attempt to comply with the Second Protocol's agreement on scheduled deliveries, the War Department instead hastily arranged to divert the flow to other available routes that, unfortunately, were longer and slower. Then, when the Soviets reinstated ALSIB route plans as abruptly as they canceled them, the flow of diverted aircraft back to Alaska could not be resumed at once, although orders were issued to restore the volume as quickly as possible.

As a result, only forty-three Lend-Lease planes were ferried to Fairbanks during the month of October—less than a third of the planned monthly total of 142.[20] The confusion caused by the hiatus not only interrupted the delivery of aircraft to the Soviets but also frustrated any attempt to relate the number of arriving aircraft to the scheduling of Soviet ferrying crews at Ladd Field.

Rising above the confusion that marred the early Northwest route delivery program, American remedial activity fortunately began to emerge. At Fairbanks, Col. Dale Gaffney returned on October 12 to relieve Col. John V. Hart[21] of his dual responsibility as commander of the CWTD and commander of Ladd Field. A few days later the CWTD, with over 350 men and forty aircraft, commenced to arrive from emergency summer dispersal bases, including Nome. ATC was immediately concerned that ATC and Soviet hangar space, offices, and barracks must be shared and might even be lost.[22] The crowded situation at Ladd Field continued to be a major problem that would require future construction and compromise. Personnel from the 6th Air Depot and the CWTD assumed a share of the work to prepare Lend-Lease planes for transfer until other arrangements were made.

At Nome, an Eleventh Air Force base squadron and related service support units arrived on October 2 to relieve the CWTD personnel departing from Marks Field. By midmonth, an ATC team from Ladd Field came in to establish an ATC presence and assist in the ferrying activities. Later, an ATC control officer and additional ATC service personnel were assigned to Nome.[23] However, the Eleventh Air Force base squadron provided most of the personnel needed to prepare Lend-Lease aircraft for crossing the Bering Sea.

Although U.S. engineer troops were introduced to quicken the Canadian contractors' construction pace on the Northwest route's string of Canadian air stations, the route was not capable of handling the volume of Lend-Lease airplanes originally planned in Washington. Other measures were urgently required. One of the most important, with a decisive effect on the future success of the ferrying operation, was the creation of the separate Alaskan Wing in the Air Transport Command's organization. Establishment of the new wing was announced on October 17. Two weeks later, on November 1, 1942, the Alaskan Wing was assigned responsibility for operating the Northwest route from Edmonton to Nome.

Col. Thomas Mosley was designated commander of the wing. He inherited the Canadian and Alaskan portions of the flimsy emergency structure that the ATC Ferrying Division and the 7th Ferrying Group had fashioned in July and August and over which only a trickle of Lend-Lease planes had passed during September and October.[24]

Mosley's wing headquarters were located at Edmonton. The nearly seven hundred men of the 7th Ferrying Group's base squadrons and detachments scattered along the route were transferred in place to the new organization. Great Falls, the processing point of entry to the Northwest route, however, continued temporarily to be a 7th Ferrying Group responsibility.[25] In addition, the mission of flying the Lend-Lease planes from Great Falls to Fairbanks continued to be assigned to the 7th Ferrying Group.[26] At a later time, pilots of the 4th Ferrying Group were attached on special duty when backlogs at Great Falls became too large for 7th Ferrying Group pilots to handle expediently.

The burden placed on Mosley to remedy the route's problems was a massive one. Except at Edmonton and Whitehorse, the Canadian stations suffered serious shortages of base facilities including housing and even sources of water, disorganized supply channels, inadequate warehousing and hangars, and insufficient trained mechanics, tools, and equipment. Therefore, service to in-transit Lend-Lease aircraft was often limited to refueling only.[27] Until the deficiencies were reduced or eliminated, the delivery of aircraft promised in the Second Protocol to the Soviets at Fairbanks was endangered.

Mosley was not a magician. Nevertheless, his enthusiasm and resourcefulness were credited with lifting morale and rescuing the wing's ferrying operation from the threat of total chaos during the depths of the worst winter weather in nearly twenty-five years.

At the same time as severe winter weather was already being heralded by temperatures plunging as low as forty degrees below zero, the Soviet requirement to winterize the Lend-Lease aircraft was being enforced. Prior to November 1, the Soviet Union, because of the urgent need for combat planes, waived the requirement. After November 1, proper winterization was mandatory on each airplane prior to its entry on the Northwest route.[28]

If winterization had been overlooked or omitted on any plane arriving at Fairbanks, the plane usually was returned to a point where the necessary specialty work could be performed. Careless servicing of planes both before and during the time they were en route to Fairbanks caused still further delays in delivery. The combination of such carelessness and the extreme cold weather in many cases resulted in broken hoses, hydraulic system failures, and electronic malfunctions.

Human factors, technical failures, and weather all contributed to slowing the ferry operation. In addition, an unforeseen backlog of aircraft clogged the logistical pipeline from factory to Great Falls.[29] These various circumstances external to and within the Alaskan Wing almost brought the Northwest route's Lend-Lease deliveries to a standstill: forty-eight aircraft arrived at Fairbanks in November but only seven arrived in December. In all four months—September through December, 1942—only 148 Lend-Lease aircraft were delivered to Fairbanks.[30]

One Lend-Lease airplane reached the Soviets in Siberia by an entirely different course. General Bradley had been well chosen for his mission to Moscow because of his patience in coping with unexpected changes in the Soviets' attitudes and decisions. From the time of his arrival in August, his patience was repeatedly tested and he established himself as the real historical "father" of the ALSIB route.

Early in November while the first Lend-Lease aircraft were flying across Siberia, Bradley and the War Department agreed that his presence in Moscow was no longer justified. Bradley obtained permission to begin his return trip via Tashkent to Chungking, China, then back to Siberia. He planned to take his B-24 bomber over the eastern portion of the ALSIB route from Yakutsk to Alaska.

Following his side trip to Chungking, Bradley encountered severe winter weather when he entered Siberia and landed at Yakutsk. Taking a rest, he scheduled his departure from Yakutsk the next night. After takeoff, Bradley's bomber soon developed engine trouble. Bradley ordered the plane back to Yakutsk. Heavy with ice and with two malfunctioning engines, the bomber barely managed to land safely. Because the engines could not be repaired at Yakutsk, Bradley and his crew remained at the air base for two weeks until arrangements were made for the Soviets to fly them to Alaska in early December.[31] The Soviet Union agreed to accept the abandoned B-24 bomber as a Lend-Lease item.

From its September beginning, the Soviet presence in Alaska gradually grew into an efficient organization of major size at Ladd Field and, to a lesser extent, at Nome. Personnel were both resident (administrators, staff, and engineers) and semitransient (pilots and crewmen). As the new ATC Alaskan Wing sought remedies for its initial inadequacies, the Soviets also rushed to develop a transfer mechanism that could accelerate the movement of the Lend-Lease aircraft through Alaska.

The Soviet Purchasing Commission civilian representatives at Ladd Field were few in number. They handled the Lend-Lease transfer documents and records. The Soviet Military Mission in Alaska, on the other hand, was much larger. Its members, all military personnel, were directly involved in the actual ferrying operation from Alaska into Siberia. In addition to commanding the military mission at Ladd Field, Colonel Machin also commanded all other Soviet military personnel in Alaska and was responsible for the ALSIB route's operations from Fairbanks through Nome to Uel'kal.

As chief of the Soviet Military Mission's technical services, Colonel Kiselev was in charge of the ground-based engineers and mechanics. To inspect and process the Lend-Lease aircraft, Kiselev used engineering technicians with expertise in the various types of bombers and fighters. Additional specialists were available to apply their knowledge in the fields of electrical equipment and circuitry, ordnance, communications, cargo, and supply. The Soviet chief engineering officer at Nome was responsible to Kiselev.

Colonel Machin's staff included an adjutant [aide], a chief of staff, and two other officers, one for communications and the other for personnel. His major operations unit was the 1st Ferrying Aviation Regiment, the commander of which had two deputies and a personnel officer.

When required by the number of Lend-Lease aircraft awaiting departure from Ladd Field, the ferrying regiment could provide pilots and crews from two bomber squadrons and three fighter squadrons, each having two flights. In addition, a transport squadron of five flights was available to serve the regiment.

At Nome, the senior ranking Soviet officer functioned through two command channels: as commander of the Soviet air base unit he was responsible to the commander of the Soviet Military Mission; as regimental navigator he was responsible to the commander of the 1st Ferrying Aviation Regiment.

Col. Michael G. Machin, commander of the Soviet Military Mission in Alaska, 1942–44. Courtesy George Kisevalter

Col. Peter S. Kiselev, chief of technical and inspection services and executive officer, Soviet Military Mission, Fairbanks. Courtesy George Kisevalter

Selected senior bomber pilots were used as "leaders of fighters." With his bomber leading the way, an experienced pilot was able to shepherd numbers of fighters to Nome and onward to the next landing field, usually Uel'kal, in eastern Siberia.[32]

Among the forty-eight aircraft delivered to Fairbanks in November, thirteen were P-39 fighters, the first of that type to be prepared to fly over the ALSIB route. Peter Gamov, commander of the 1st Bomber Squadron, was also a designated leader of fighters. In late November, Gamov departed Ladd Field in his B-25 bomber with ten P-39 fighters following him. From Nome, Gamov continued to lead his covey of fighters across the Bering Sea toward Uel'kal. Too late, Gamov learned by radio that Uel'kal was fog-shrouded. An unfinished Soviet airstrip was located south of the Bering Strait near Cape Chaplino. When Gamov learned that the airstrip was fog-free, he weighed odds of the gamble and then decided to divert the entire flight and risk a landing there. Fortunately, all eleven airplanes managed to come in safely despite the airstrip's condition. The next morning, with favorable weather now reported at Uel'kal, Gamov summoned a transport plane loaded with heaters to warm the engines of the grounded aircraft, after which his party flew on to Uel'kal.

Not long afterward, five C-47 transports were loaded at Ladd Field for an emergency flight to take a special load of high explosives across Siberia en route to the war front. Gamov volunteered to pilot one of the transports as far as Uel'kal. On the approach to Uel'kal in frigid winter temperatures, Gamov's cockpit windshield iced over and the transport's pitotstatic tube air speed indicator froze. Flying blind and having no idea of his craft's air speed, Gamov knew that his C-47 was in serious trouble. Pounding frantically, he managed to break a hole in the windshield. Through the hole he glimpsed the whirling ground as the plane plunged wildly out of control. He struggled to regain control of the C-47 by using full throttle. Peeking through the broken windshield, Gamov was able to land the explosives-laden transport at Uel'kal without mishap.

Questioning Gamov about his narrow escape, Colonel Machin asked whether he had forgotten to heat the pitotstatic tube air speed indicator before taking off; heating the tube reduced the likelihood of it freezing. Gamov denied "forgetting." Not having flown a C-47 before, he was not familiar with the peculiarities of the indicator. After Gamov's admission, Machin ordered him to begin pilot transition training not only for C-47 transports but for P-39 fighters as well.

In the meantime, an A-20 bomber crash-landed on its belly in a rough beach area about twenty miles from Nome. Following the landing, American technicians succeeded in repairing the bomber and declared it fit to fly. Unfortunately, deep snow covered the beach so that a takeoff was not feasible. Since the bomber had already been transferred to the Soviets, American advisors suggested to the Soviets that the bomber be dismantled and used for spare parts. ALSIB route commander Colonel

Mazuruk, accompanied by Peter Gamov, arrived at Nome before any action was taken at the crash site, and together they visited the snowbound A-20. "I can fly it," Gamov promised. Although skeptical, Mazuruk agreed to allow Gamov to make the attempt.

With the help of a military vehicle, Gamov taxied the bomber through deep snow until they found a solid strip of ice about two thousand feet long on the beach. Gamov volunteered to risk a takeoff on the icy runway. He wrestled the bomber into the air barely in time to avoid crashing in the sea.[33]

During his lengthy tour of ALSIB duty in Alaska, Gamov was distinguished by his daring, resourcefulness, and flying skill, all of which continued to be demonstrated in close brushes with possible crashes and death (chap. 6).

The situation in which the Alaskan Wing found itself in late 1942 was a critical one. At that time, whether the Northwest route could have handled any additional aircraft was questionable. However, even as steps were being taken to ease the backlogs of aircraft from the factories and rectify the logistical confusion that dogged the route all the way to Fairbanks, early disputes arose between the United States and the Soviet Union over the meaning of *delivered*. By protocol arrangement, the Soviets indicated the types and numbers of planes required. The United States considered the aircraft to have been "delivered" when they emerged from the factories. *Nyet*, said the Soviets. They did not consider any plane delivered until it had been passed into Soviet hands.[34]

In addition to being unwilling to accept the American way of accounting, the Soviets also complained that deliveries to the Fairbanks point of transfer remained behind schedule. The time difference between delivery at the factories and delivery at Fairbanks accounted for some of the delay. Many weeks were spent in moving a factory-new plane to Great Falls. Here it was given a final processing before clearance for a ferrying pilot to fly it over the Northwest route to Fairbanks. Up to two weeks could be required for Alaskan Wing inspectors and mechanics to certify that a plane was ready for transfer. And then the Soviet Military Mission undertook its own inspection before accepting the craft.[35]

In all, factories produced 14,798 airplanes for the Soviet Union. Of these, 690 were lost en route to the Soviet Union. The remaining 14,108 arrived via various Lend-Lease routes, including the ALSIB.[36] Regarding the delivery via Alaska, the factories manufactured 8,057 airplanes, but 133 were lost in the United States and Canada in the process of being ferried to Fairbanks. The Soviets accepted 7,924 (appendix A).

Brig. Gen. Dale V. Gaffney, commander of the Alaskan Wing, Air Transport Command, with Col. Nikifor S. Vasin, commander of the 1st Ferrying Aviation Regiment. Courtesy Col. Louis Klam

After the low point in the flow of aircraft to Fairbanks in December, 1942, deliveries started to increase dramatically. More than four hundred planes had arrived at the transfer point by the end of March. The goal of 142 planes per month was reached and then exceeded in April. By the June 30 end of the Second Protocol period, 1,107 aircraft had been delivered; the original goal had been 1,704.[37]

Colonel Mosley's efforts to remedy the ATC Alaskan Wing's aircraft maintenance and related problems on the Northwest route obviously improved the route's performance to some degree. However, Mosley's primary effort was aimed at plans for converting the ATC wing permanently into a truly efficient ferrying organization. Unexpectedly in April, before Mosley could translate his plans into action, he was reassigned to North Africa.[38]

Colonel Gaffney, the commander of CWTD and Ladd Field, succeeded Mosley as the ATC wing commander on May 8, 1943. He soon was promoted to brigadier general. By reason of his new assignment, Gaffney automatically was relieved of command of the CWTD but for a short time retained personal command of Ladd Field.

Relying on Mosley's concepts, Gaffney launched a vigorous and successful reorganization that guided his ATC wing's ferrying operations for the rest of the war. Beginning in May, all of the Alaskan air stations involved in the ATC ferrying mission passed to ATC control. First, the Alaska Defense Command, having already recognized that ATC had the only mission of significance at Galena, Big Delta, Northway, and Tanacross, agreed to release the bases and their service troops to ATC.[39] Next, because of increasing demands for air support in the Aleutian Islands offensive, the Eleventh Air Force removed its personnel from Nome's Marks Field in June, leaving ATC's sixty-man detachment with the total responsibility for performing any necessary service on ALSIB route aircraft. The Eleventh Air Force void was soon filled by ATC transfers from other points, with the entire enlarged ATC detachment under the command of Lt. Col. Richard Hackford.[40] And finally, Ladd Field was transferred to ATC's exclusive jurisdiction, together with Ladd Field's various air force units involved in the ALSIB route mission. Gaffney handpicked Col. Russell Keillor as Ladd Field's new commander.[41]

Outside Alaska, the ATC wing's reorganization later brought all of the various stations on the Northwest route under the wing's direct control. Among them was East Base at Great Falls, where all Lend-Lease aircraft destined for Ladd Field were processed. In addition, three Army Air Force service squadrons were assigned to the wing, one each for Edmonton, Whitehorse, and Nome.[42]

The primitive conditions at the more remote bases on the Northwest route remained a serious bottleneck during the first twelve months of ALSIB route operation. Although every major base had at least one usable runway in the autumn of 1942, other bases such as those at Fort Nelson, Watson Lake, and Northway required another year to be equipped with sufficient facilities to handle the increasing ferry traffic.[43]

In due time, the ATC's acquisition and reorganization of Northwest route facilities and units would produce the wing's desired results, but a satisfactory flow of Lend-Lease planes to Fairbanks was not reached until the Third Protocol deliveries began after July 1, 1943.

5.
Face-to-Face

As the winter of 1942–43 advanced and the initial difficulties servicing the route and ensuring a sufficient flow of aircraft began to smooth out, delivering planes to Alaska was an accepted American obligation. Ferrying the same aircraft from Alaska across Siberia became a Soviet responsibility. The vital connection between the end of the Northwest route and the start of the ALSIB route was Fairbanks (Ladd Field). The joining of the two routes at this location, however, represented much more than the mere point of transfer of aircraft ownership. Here, in mid-Alaska, the connection brought together two cultures so different that relations were persistently fraught with the uncertainty created by opposing political and economic perspectives.

Nevertheless, the United States and the Soviet Union were allied against a common enemy, and Americans and Soviets in Alaska were pledged to cooperate.

In the absence of a common language, the first step in achieving cooperation was establishing the means to reduce the communication barrier.

In the beginning, the available linguists, both Soviet and American, were scant. The Soviet Purchasing Commission delegation at Ladd Field arrived with a Russian translator, and the Soviet Military Mission cadre brought two English-speaking technical interpreters. When the ATC established its base at Ladd Field, two Russian-speaking civilian technical interpreters arrived to reinforce the efforts of a few air force personnel who spoke Russian. As the ALSIB route operation expanded, so did the need for linguists.

In the United States, qualified Russian linguists of military age were not easily identified, and the language schools were unprepared to fill the personnel pipeline with acceptable graduates. Many of the Russian-speaking military candidates who were found for Alaskan duty were offspring either of immigrants from Czarist Russia or of White Russians who had escaped from Russia during the Red Revolution.[1] Some of the older linguists were themselves veterans of the defeated White Army.

Most of the American ALSIB route Russian-language interpreters and liaison officers therefore had Russian names and were either anti-Soviet by family orientation or they had personal reasons for harboring anti-Soviet sentiments. However, they followed orders and performed their duties efficiently and without outward rancor. Igor Gubert, who was to become a liaison officer, said he liked some of the Soviets as individuals, but "I could not forget that they were representatives of a regime that killed my relatives and friends and robbed me of my original national identity."[2] Although the future interpreters and liaison officers no longer had close family ties in the Soviet Union,[3] their Russian family names were not overlooked by the alert Soviet Military Mission (chap. 6).

The War Department assigned to the Alaska Defense Command, already responsible for military intelligence operations in Alaska, responsibility for conduct of the official foreign liaison with Soviet personnel. The Alaska Defense Command was also charged with maintaining records of the entrance and departure of Soviet air ferry personnel as well as with monitoring their activities while in Alaska.[4] However, the ultimate objective of the official foreign liaison program was to lend all possible assistance to operations and expedite the movement of Lend-Lease aircraft through Alaska.

The ATC Alaskan Wing had technical interpreters who, of course, also had a primary objective of contributing to the successful operation of the ALSIB route. The ATC wing once ambitiously planned to use a pool of sixty technical interpreters for duty in Alaska[5] but was in fact able to obtain only a handful. The two groups of American specialists—foreign liaison interpreters and ATC technical interpreters—unofficially ignored their separate sources of authority. Out of necessity, they shared their linguistic talents for the sake of the common objective, and the Soviets were the ultimate beneficiaries.

To organize unique language specialists into a body to meet tactical as well as foreign liaison requirements, the Alaska Defense Command created a combined Interpreters and Interrogators (I&I) Detachment.[6] Japanese-speaking linguists were in the Interrogators section for service in the Aleutian Islands combat zone, and the foreign liaison Interpreters section comprised Russian-speaking officers and noncommissioned officers destined for ALSIB route service. Although four foreign liaison officers and sixteen sergeant-interpreters were authorized, the actual number in the I&I Russian section fluctuated due to personnel transfers and the uneven availability of qualified replacements during the ALSIB route's life span.

Most of the I&I interpreters were posted to Fairbanks and Nome. In general, their activities were controlled from the I&I offices established at each base for the convenience of and assistance to pilots and engineers of the Soviet Military Mission. Whenever Soviet ferry operations warranted their presence, selected I&I interpreters were sent to the alternate ALSIB route bases in Alaska at Galena and Moses Point.

At Ladd Field, the focal point was the Base Foreign Liaison Office.[7] American liaison officers later recalled that "the office was a sort of embassy where Soviets and Americans could meet. We had to handle everything ranging from arguments over aircraft to small housekeeping details. We also acted as a consulate, keeping track of the names of Soviets coming in and out of Alaska." At Nome, the liaison office was referred to as the Russian-American Bureau of Information.[8]

I&I personnel were placed in the traffic control towers of the air bases at both Ladd Field and Nome to interpret instructions for Soviet aircraft landings and takeoffs. I&I interpreters were available when needed to bridge the language gap between U.S. and Soviet mechanics as they serviced Lend-Lease aircraft for ALSIB route passage. In addition, the liaison officers arranged and interpreted discussions between senior American and Soviet officials. On special occasions, I&I personnel were designated as American interpreter-escorts to accompany Soviet diplomatic or military groups passing through Alaska bound for the continental United States.[9]

Until permanent I&I personnel arrived singly or in groups for duty in 1943, a temporary liaison program at Ladd Field was supervised by Lt. Col. Walter Chuinski, on temporary duty from the Western Defense Command.[10] The interim liaison operation at Nome was directed by Lt. Thaddius Krolicki, aide to the commanding general of the Nome army garrison.[11]

Capt. George G. Kisevalter was the organizer and first commander of the I&I Russian section; he later became the first chief liaison officer at Fairbanks.[12] Despite the difficulties encountered in working with a frustrated American air transport command and a cautious Soviet military mission, Kisevalter established the foreign liaison pattern for his subordinates and successor to use.

Captain Kisevalter was born in St. Petersburg, Russia, in 1910. His father was a respected engineer whose range of expertise included the development and manufacture of munitions. His French mother was a multilingual teacher of Russian, French, German, and English.

With the advent of World War I, the Russian government's various ministries created purchasing commissions in the United States to secure supplies and equipment and then ship them via Seattle across the Pacific Ocean to Vladivostok. The War Ministry sent the elder Kisevalter, accompanied by his wife and son, to join its purchasing commission and establish a munitions factory to supply artillery shells for the Russian army. The factory, operating under the name of the Eddystone Ammunition Corporation, was located at Eddystone, Pennsylvania, near Chester on the Delaware River. The corporation also leased swampland across the river in New Jersey for use as an artillery shell proving ground.

Following the American entry into the war and the collapse of the Russian imperial government in 1917, the U.S. government continued the munitions plant operation and used the New Jersey proving ground (later to become the site of Fort Dix). During the short-lived Kerensky government, American-made munitions made their way to Vladivostok, whence anti-Bolshevik armies later used them in Siberia.

Their relatives in Russia having been killed or scattered during the Red Revolution, the Kisevalters became naturalized American citizens. However, the parents ensured that their son retained his fluency in Russian. George also acquired a knowledge of French and German and accompanied his mother on European travels in 1925.

Kisevalter attended Dartmouth College, where he received his engineering master's degree in 1931. He then worked for a consulting engineering firm on construction of the New York City circumferencial parkway. During this period he became a licensed New York state professional engineer and at the same time earned a commission as an Army Corps of Engineers reserve officer.

In 1941, Kisevalter was ordered to active military duty. He was assigned to the 42nd Engineer Battalion and later became the unit's adjutant. After the battalion was sent to the Aleutian Islands, Captain Kisevalter was put in charge of constructing the long-postponed early warning radar station on Unalaska near Dutch Harbor. The project was hardly under way when the Japanese attacked Dutch Harbor in June, 1942.

During Kisevalter's sojourn at the construction site, Brig. Gen. Edgar Colladay, the army commander at Fort Mears (Dutch Harbor), learned that Kisevalter spoke Russian. "A flotilla of Soviet submarines passed through Dutch Harbor," Kisevalter recalled. "They were en route, two at a time, from the Soviet Far East to the Panama Canal, then via the Bahamas to Scapa Flow in Scotland, and on to Murmansk [on the USSR's Arctic coast]," he said. General Colladay, scheduled to make a courtesy call on board one of the submarines, asked Kisevalter to accompany him and Dutch Harbor navy officers to act as an interpreter. "After our visit, the submarine was refueled and dispatched in the direction of the Canal. . . . It was all a very friendly encounter," Kisevalter noted.

In early 1943, after the radar station was completed and operational, the Alaska Defense Command, now aware of Kisevalter's language expertise, arranged for his assignment to its Fort Richardson headquarters. Kisevalter was immediately put to work on engineering intelligence studies and related monographs concerning the Soviets' adjacent Komandorski Islands as well as the Kamchatka and Chukotski peninsulas.

On June 1, 1943, he was named the commanding officer of the Alaska Defense Command's new I&I Russian section. He formally assumed command three days later, and the assignment ended his military engineering career.

To integrate the I&I interpreters into the Soviet-American liaison operation, Kisevalter conducted his first survey of the key bases in June. Other visits followed. Adjustments were made to insure that the best qualified interpreters were properly located. Kisevalter himself settled at Ladd Field in November, 1943, to assume his additional duty as the ALSIB route's chief liaison officer.

Michael B. Gavrisheff was one of the original officers in the I&I foreign liaison organization.[13] His family roots were in Russia as well as in Russian America. His Russian ancestors were cossacks who entered Peter the Great's navy service at the time when Vitus Bering was also recruited. His great grandfather's brother was Login O. Gavrishev, the last lieutenant governor of Russian America, 1863–67. A senior navy officer in the service of the Russian American Company, Gavrishev had been stunned by Russia's abandonment of Alaska and was among the first of the disillusioned Russians to depart Sitka immediately after the formal transfer of Alaska to the United States in 1867. He retired from the Russian navy with the rank of rear admiral. The original *Gavrishev* family name, through transliteration into German, has since become *Gavrisheff* in English.

Boris Gavrisheff, Michael's father, graduated from the Russian naval

Left to right: Lieutenant Gabelia, ATC Russian-speaking officer; Captain Kisevalter, Captain Gavrisheff, and Lieutenant de Shishmareff, assigned to I&I Russian section in early 1944. Courtesy George Kisevalter

academy in 1905. Following his obligatory tour of service as a navy officer, he requested a transfer to the reserve fleet in order to pursue a master's degree and a career in topographical engineering. When World War I erupted in 1914, Boris Gavrisheff returned to active duty and commanded PT-type navy craft that raided German installations on the Baltic Sea coast. Twice wounded, he received one of the czar's highest decorations, the Arms of St. George. He later commanded a squadron of mine sweepers.

Boris Gavrisheff's son Michael was born in 1917 in the midst of St. Petersburg's revolutionary turmoil. In 1918, still loyal to the captive czar and his life threatened by his rebellious sailors, Boris decided that it was time to leave. He escaped from St. Petersburg across Siberia to Vladivostok. Although Bolshevik forces did not yet endanger Vladivostok, Boris anticipated his need to leave his temporary refuge. He managed to send word for his wife and infant son to join him. With her baby in her arms, Michael's mother, only twenty-seven years old and born a Polish countess, abandoned her home in strife-torn St. Petersburg and made the Siberian railroad crossing. Reunited, the family sailed for Japan.

The Gavrisheffs, soon to become four with the birth of a daughter, lived first in Kobe and then in Yokohama. Michael, six years old in 1923, recalled the catastrophic earthquake that damaged the city. "I still remember our sitting on top of a hill overlooking Yokohama harbor with an umbrella over our heads in a driving rain all night long."

Shortly thereafter, although they had obtained visas to enter the United States, the Gavrisheffs decided instead to go to Mexico, where they lived until 1932 when they resettled permanently in San Antonio, Texas. Boris was employed in various occupations in Mexico, including construction and petroleum engineering. In San Antonio, however, he entered a new engineering field as the chief engineer for Edgar Tobin Aerial Surveys, a pioneer firm engaged in aerial mapping.

Michael Gavrisheff, fluent in Russian, Spanish, and English, graduated from high school in San Antonio in 1935. He enrolled first in Texas A&M College and later in St. Mary's University, the latter located in San Antonio. "During summers after my senior year in high school and then during college," Gavrisheff related, "I was fortunate to work as an engineering aide to my father and later on my own as a map compiler, photographic dark room technician and an engineering assistant."

In 1940, because he was a member of a Texas national guard infantry unit scheduled for extended active military service, Gavrisheff instead enlisted in the regular army air corps. When the United States entered the war, he applied for engineer officer training and was commissioned a second lieutenant and assigned, probably because of his civilian experience, to a topographical engineering battalion in May, 1942. But his career in military mapping ended abruptly in December, when he was ordered to report to the Pentagon so that his fluency in Russian could be tested. "I was interviewed by a Russian-speaking scientist at the Smithsonian Institution," Gavrisheff said.

Apparently the War Department was satisfied with the test results because Gavrisheff was ordered to go to San Francisco on January 1, 1943, for orientation at the headquarters of the Western Defense Command. Later in January, he was issued orders to proceed to Alaska. On arriving at Fort Richardson, he met and worked with Colonel Choinski and later with Captain Kisevalter while the I&I Russian section was being assembled.

In late April, Gavrisheff and three enlisted interpreters went to Ladd Field as the nucleus of the unique wartime liaison operation. Gavrisheff remained at his Ladd Field post for two years. As a persuasive liaison officer, he earned acceptance and respect from ATC Alaskan Wing and Soviet officials alike. Later, as Kisevalter's deputy, he helped the expanding liaison program through its period of growing pains, and finally, he succeeded Kisevalter as chief liaison officer in 1944.

Igor A. Gubert, also a young man of Russian birth, was the I&I Russian section's first and only foreign liaison officer-in-charge at Nome during the war.[14]

Until 1937, however, Gubert had been a man without a country. He was the son of Alexander Goubareff, an officer and specialist in communications in the Russian army. Goubareff in 1916 was transferred from St. Petersburg to Harbin, Manchuria, to establish a military wireless radio station there. At the time of his father's departure for his Manchurian assignment, Igor was a newborn infant, and he and his mother remained at their St. Petersburg home. A year later, in the midst of the revolutionary upheaval, mother and baby left St. Petersburg and undertook the five-thousand-mile journey to Harbin.

Because of the wartime chaos in St. Petersburg, Igor's mother was unable to obtain a legitimate birth record to identify the infant boy. Later, Igor's parents in Harbin filed papers claiming that Igor was actually born in Manchuria in 1917. This legal fabrication not only made Igor a Chinese citizen but pegged him at one year younger than his actual age.

In 1921, during the flood of thousands of White Russian refugees from Siberia into and through Manchuria, Igor's parents divorced. Alexander Goubareff, now a civilian employed by the Chinese Eastern Railroad, remarried. Alexander and his new family as well as Igor and his mother had no choice but to adapt to life in the turbulent Russian colony in Harbin.

Igor attended Russian schools and later concentrated on engineering studies at Harbin's Polytechnic Institute. However, life amidst the mêlée of Japanese, Chinese, White Russian, and Soviet political and economic intrigue and instability became intolerable for him. Dreaming of going to the United States, he regularly applied for an American entry visa, but he was repeatedly disappointed. "The U.S. immigration quota from Manchuria was limited to one hundred Chinese per year," he said. Igor's father and his new family were luckier: they were permitted to immigrate to the United States in 1934.

"Then, on my twentieth [Russian] birthday on a cold 1936 December morning, I received my visa in a letter from the American consulate. I'll never forget that day!" he said. Leaving his mother in Harbin, he soon sailed for California. Also remaining in Harbin was Alla Madievsky, a schoolmate whom he had known casually for two years. He never expected to encounter Alla again. "When I landed in San Francisco on February 14, 1937, my new life began!" he said.

Igor's mother remained in Harbin for another year. When a Soviet-Japanese border war seemed inevitable, she moved from Manchuria to join other Russian refugees in Shanghai, where she managed to survive during the coming war years. "When President Roosevelt declared an oil embargo against Japan, it was clear to me that war with Japan was coming, and soon," Igor explained. "I gathered all the money I had [$400] and sent it to my mother in Shanghai. She used the money to buy kerosene. She stored the kerosene in five-gallon cans in her room. She traded small amounts of kerosene for food."

In San Francisco, the gathering of war clouds in 1939 found Igor Goubareff adapting to his new home and country. He worked as a part-time janitor while studying engineering at the University of California at Berkeley. He also found friends in the San Francisco Russian immigrant colony.

With the help of relatives already in California, Alla Madievsky arrived in San Francisco in 1939, and her mother followed a year later. Alla's father, Col. Anatole Madievsky, who was involved in Gen. Grigorii Semenov's anti-Soviet paramilitary organization, remained in Manchuria.[15] Alla never saw him again (chap. 10).

Igor said he would not have known that Alla was in San Francisco had it not been for the jealousy of a female friend. Somebody told her that Igor's "fiancée" had arrived from Harbin. Igor denied any knowledge. In a fit of pique, she produced a piece of paper with a telephone number written on it. "Here," she said, "call her!" Puzzled but curious, Igor made the call and found himself back in touch with Alla.

From that beginning, the two Russian immigrants became reacquainted, and the sense of impending war perhaps fueled their relationship throughout 1940. Military mobilization commenced. At the close of the fall semester at the University of California, Igor decided that "my country needed me," he said. In February, 1941, he enlisted in the army.

Following basic training, Private Igor A. Goubareff received his cherished American citizenship papers at Fort Ord, California. "My family name was frequently mispronounced and was not easy to spell," he explained. He used the acceptance of his new citizenship to take a shorter, uncomplicated name. "And so Igor A. *Gubert* was born!"

Gubert was sent to Camp Davis, North Carolina, for officer candidate schooling in August, 1942. In late October, on the eve of being commissioned a second lieutenant, he sent a telegram to Alla urging her to come at once. Immediately following his graduation on November 5, Lieutenant Gubert was given a short leave of absence, and he and Alla were married. He then was placed in an officers' replacement pool for prompt overseas assignment.

On December 15, however, he was unexpectedly ordered to the Pentagon for Russian language fluency testing. After his Washington interview, he learned that he was bound for duty in Alaska. He left his bride in San Francisco; they would not see each another again for two years.

Destined for service with the future I&I Russian section, Gubert reported to Fort Richardson, Alaska. In April, 1943, he was selected to go to Nome with a mission to reduce rising tensions between Soviets and Americans there. Told that his assignment was a temporary one, he did not take his winter clothing. Finally, in late August when it became apparent that his presence in Nome would be more extended, he asked for his winter wardrobe. Unknown to Gubert at that time, his highly effective foreign liaison talents would keep him at Nome not only during the approaching winter but throughout the war.

David Chavchavadze was a descendant of Catherine the Great and Czar Nicholas I of Russia and of George XII, the last king of Georgia. Therefore by heritage, he possessed a legitimate title of prince. He was the youngest of the officers assigned to the I&I Russian section. However, he earned his army officer's commission only after serving as an enlisted interpreter in Alaska.[16]

Unlike his fellow liaison officers, David Chavchavadze was not born in Russia. His mother was Princess Nina (Romanov). The daughter of Grand Duke George Mikhailovich of Russia and Princess Marie of Greece, Nina was born in 1901 and reared in Greece and the Russian Crimea until 1914. Two months before the outbreak of World War I, her mother decided to take Nina and Nina's sister Xenia on an extended visit to England. Mother and daughters were trapped, unable to return to Russia because of the war and the subsequent revolution. They never saw their husband and father, Grand Duke George Mikhailovich, again. David Chavchavadze's maternal grandfather was among the last of the Romanov grand dukes executed by the Bolsheviks in 1919.

David's other grandfather was Prince Alexander Chavchavadze of Georgia and his grandmother was Marie Rodzianko, a Russian. Their offspring, including David's father, Prince Paul, were the first Chavchavadzes to have their Georgian blood mixed with Russian. Paul was born in St. Petersburg in 1899. Family instability finally resulted in the par-

Nome liaison office. *Left to right:* Sergeant Levitsky, Captain Gubert, and Sergeants Remneff and Garcavy. Courtesy Igor Gubert

ents' divorce. In 1914–17 during World War I, Prince Alexander was commander of a Caucasian cavalry regiment on the Austro-Hungarian front, then he returned to Georgia when the revolution started. Paul's divorced mother managed to move her children from St. Petersburg to Roumania, thereby escaping the worst of the revolutionary terror. Paul's father was not as fortunate. Brushing aside Georgia's bid for independence in 1918–21, the conquering Red Army crushed resistance in Georgia and arrested Prince Alexander. After being held in prison for ten years, he was finally executed in 1931.

David Chavchavadze thus lost both grandfathers to revolutionary firing squads.

David's mother and father, Princess Nina and Prince Paul, met in England in 1922 and married. David, an only child, was born in England in 1924. Three years later, Paul Chavchavadze was offered employment with the Cunard steamship line in the company's New York offices, and the family immigrated to the United States. With them came Vera Nagovsky, David's Russian-born and -educated nurse and governess, who devoted thirteen years to his welfare and early education. She taught him the Russian language, both spoken and written. "She, more than anyone else, put Russia in me," David said.

In 1938, he entered boarding school at Andover and was graduated four years later. He went to Yale University on scholarship in 1942 and at the same time joined the army enlisted reserve. He was called to active duty in February, 1943.

Private David Chavchavadze completed two months of basic training at Camp Croft, South Carolina. Then the Pentagon's relentless search for Russian-speaking personnel located and transferred him to the Military Intelligence Training Center, Camp Ritchie, Maryland. After alternating between training exercises and fatigue duty ("kitchen police"), David and six other Russian-speaking enlisted men were abruptly promoted from private to sergeant and assigned to Alaskan duty. An uneventful trip by train and ship brought them to Fort Richardson, where they joined the I&I Russian section and were sent to Fairbanks. They arrived at Ladd Field in late November, 1943.

For Sgt. David Chavchavadze, his on-the-job training to be an army foreign liaison officer with major responsibilities was just beginning.

The third and last chief liaison officer and the last I&I Russian section commander was Eugene de Moore,[17] who succeeded Michael Gavrisheff in April, 1945. When de Moore arrived at Fairbanks, the war in Europe was ending and the ALSIB route's ferrying life was within five months of conclusion. Given his late appearance on the ALSIB scene, de Moore in effect arrived in time to turn off the lights and lock the doors of the Base Foreign Liaison Office at Ladd Field.

Born in Russia soon after 1900, de Moore is known to have been a cadet in General Wrangel's White Army and was in combat in the Crimea in 1920 during the civil war. When Wrangel's army collapsed, de Moore escaped into Turkey and eventually came to the United States. His original Russian surname may have been Muraviev.

Most of the I&I Russian section's enlisted liaison interpreters remained at their Alaskan posts throughout the war. Others, however, for various reasons, served for shorter periods before being transferred. Three men qualified for officer candidate schooling and never returned to Alaska. Two unqualified officers also came and went quickly.

Responsible to George Kisevalter, Michael Gavrisheff, Igor Gubert, David Chavchavadze, or Eugene de Moore, the American interpreters who were face-to-face with members of the Soviet Military Mission and in-transit Soviet officials and civilians[18] included several whose recent

Russian derivation is known: Nicholas Baranoff, a veteran of General Wrangel's White Army that the Bolsheviks defeated in the Crimea—Baranoff also escaped to Turkey in 1920; Paul Duncan, whose Scottish ancestors settled in Russia at the time of Peter the Great; Leonard Gmirkin, one of the sons of a White Russian family living in China—Leonard and his brother Vasia were kidnapped as children by brigands in Sinkiang Province and held for ransom; Valerian Postovsky, who as a passenger aboard a B-17 bomber flying from Nome to Moses Point parachuted to safety after the bomber caught fire in midflight; and Victor Salatco, Igor Gubert's classmate at the Polytechnic Institute in Harbin, Manchuria.

Other U. S. interpreters, their surnames sounding just as Russian but in some cases their first names unknown (FNU), included: FNU Bleichman, Ilya Bolotovsky, FNU Bryner, John Carpyna, Anatole Chelnov, Mitchell Daniloff, Demetrius Dviochenko-Markov, Vladimir Farafontoff, Andrew Federoff, George Garcavy, Alexander Homonchuck, Vsevolod Levitsky, Vassily Mihailov, Vladimir Pekarsky, Nicholas Rankov, FNU Remneff, FNU Remy, George de Timofeyev, Boris Tumarin and Ilya Wolston.

6.
The Invisible Barrier

When first brought face-to-face in Alaska, most Americans and Soviets had little in common. Americans understood that the Soviets were engaged in a struggle with the Germans for their national survival. They also understood that the Americans and Soviets were allies against Germany, and that after the U.S. government offered to bolster the Soviet defenders with Lend-Lease help, the ALSIB route became one special avenue for expediting that help. Nonetheless, because until recently they had considered the Soviet Union a menace, most Americans approached the Soviets in Alaska with a degree of uncertainty.

For their part, the Soviets were schooled in Russian history, which is replete with examples of treachery by foreigners. Even though Soviet military and civilian personnel were guests in Alaska, the Soviets' inherited national suspicion of all foreigners applied to Americans in Alaska, too.[1] Suspicion was an invisible barrier, making cautious Americans and wary Soviets unlikely candidates for enthusiastic cohesion.

From the time of their arrival in Alaska, Soviet officials tried to place general restrictions on Soviet social fraternization with Americans[2] and issued definite orders against mingling with American women. Soviet unit commanders who enforced discipline were themselves held responsible for flaws in their men's individual behavior. Soviets who spoke or understood English were often advised to conceal this from the Americans.

Some of the senior Soviet officers visiting Nome from Siberia were reported to be wearing junior officer insignia to divert American attention.[3]

Until American I&I liaison interpreters arrived to penetrate the language barrier, the Soviets avoided off-duty contact with Americans, a practice probably inspired by NKVD surveillance. Although the Soviet enlisted men watched Americans play baseball, they showed no desire to become involved. Instead they played soccer among themselves. The officers preferred using their own club room in the basement of the Soviet officers' quarters rather than joining the Americans in the larger Soviet-American club facilities.[4]

The I&I liaison interpreters came under instant pressure to convince the Soviets of their sincerity and desire to be helpful.

An I&I Russian section letter of instruction was circulated to orient new interpreter personnel concerning their role in improving Soviet-American relations:

It is necessary that you perform these [liaison] duties with the utmost diligence, care and discretion. You must be on the friendliest terms with the personnel of the Red Army [i.e., Red Air Force], cultivating their friendship carefully and bearing in mind that friendship is won slowly and "forcing" oneself on someone most assuredly will result in apathy. You must be careful in your military courtesy toward our own and foreign officers. Always strive to [gain] respect toward yourself. . . . Do not try to make yourself seem important; the quieter and more efficient you are, the better you will get along with everyone and the more respect you will command from all concerned.[5]

The liaison interpreters confronted the invisible barrier and began to make progress, especially at the working level, where American and Soviet mechanics, using interpreter assistance, developed an excellent relationship.[6] The polite and well-behaved Soviets as a group displayed a formal face in their official contacts with Americans. However, on an individual basis they soon commenced to speak on personal subjects. They voiced some of their anxieties and frustrations in connection with their duties and discussed their concern for the safety and well-being of surviving family members endangered by the war. Some of them expressed wishes to be transferred to other ALSIB route bases in Siberia, where vodka was readily available and where they could associate with Soviet women.[7] Otherwise, they were reluctant to be involved in any controversial topic.[8]

The subject of the Soviet Union's relationship with Japan was one that the Soviets in Alaska originally sought to ignore.[9] In 1943, Japan was making ominous radio broadcasts issuing threats and warning the Soviet Union against putting Siberian bases at the disposal of the United States.[10] Soviets also avoided discussions touching on the Soviet-Japanese neutrality concord.[11]

Soviet personnel never showed the slightest interest in discussing the communist theory of world revolution, nor did they attempt to disseminate communist propaganda during their three-year residence in Fairbanks and Nome. American liaison officers learned that the Soviets were aware that any hint of such activity would endanger the Lend-Lease cooperative program. In May, 1943, Soviets expressed surprise when Moscow announced the dissolution of the Comintern but made no further comment. Subsequently, they remained consistently silent on the subject.[12]

Although not planned primarily to placate Americans, a new style of Russian military uniform dimmed the visual flaunting of Bolshevik symbolism in Alaska. In one of the initiatives to rally the Soviet people against German invasion, the Kremlin resurrected the images of "Holy Mother Russia" and the "Great Russian Nation." To reflect the change, the new uniform was introduced, and it appeared in Alaska for the first time in March, 1943. The design changes were subtle ones involving a new blouse and the relocation of military insignia from the collar to shoulder boards, both reminiscent of the styling used in the former Imperial Russian army uniforms. The symbolism recalling the pre-revolutionary past was carefully noted in both Fairbanks and Nome. Some of the dedicated Soviet officials in Alaska, including Colonel Machin, were slow in accepting the changes. Machin delayed wearing the new uniform for several months before capitulating.[13]

Officers of the Soviet Military Mission, while they appeared to welcome the services of American personnel, made no early effort to develop casual friendships with American counterparts.

Nor was there any Soviet-American effort to perpetuate friendly contacts between American pilots on the Northwest route and Soviet pilots on the ALSIB route. The two groups of pilots concentrated on the aircraft that they were flying and not on one another. Soviet airmen responded to the urgency of ferrying as many aircraft as soon as possible from Alaska to the war front. American pilots realized that their aircraft deliveries to Ladd Field were important, but their personal involvement in the war seemed too remote to share with the Soviets. The irregularity of their respective flight schedules also contributed to the invisible barrier. Having once met at Ladd Field, the likelihood that the same two American and Soviet pilots would share a bottle of vodka there again was slim.

Based on whatever infrequent contact they had with Soviet airmen at Ladd Field, many of the American pilots from the Northwest route regarded the ALSIB route pilots as being somewhat arrogant and cavalier about their flying ability, even to the point of being habitually reckless.[14]

The Soviet pilots were on balance older than their American counterparts, and many of them were veterans recently disengaged from combat with German foes. Some of them, including Lt. Col. Nikifor Vasin, had survived the *taran*—the act of deliberately ramming enemy aircraft. Others, having downed numerous enemy planes, were recognized as aces. The evidence of their battlefield heroics was displayed in decorations and ribbons that they wore at Ladd Field.

At Nome the Soviet-American relationship proved to be unique. During the winter of 1942–43, Nome's facilities for the Soviets' use were inadequate and awaited improvement through new construction. The Eleventh Air Force base unit and the ATC representatives at Marks Field managed to provide for the transient Soviets and their aircraft bound for Siberia, but the general situation became progressively more strained. Soviets, both transient and permanent, reacted coolly because, they said, they were not welcome at Nome.

Fortunately, the timely combined presence of two American officers reassured the Soviets and eased the strain on Soviet-American relations. Lt. Igor Gubert arrived to organize the official liaison operations, and Brig. Gen. Edwin Jones, the Nome garrison commander, revealed an extraordinary flair for international diplomacy. Together, Gubert and Jones brushed aside the veil that concealed a worsening situation.

Gubert spent the spring and summer of 1943 expanding a liaison organization that originally included two enlisted Russian-language interpreters but soon grew to six. By midsummer, Michael Gavrisheff visited Nome on behalf of George Kisevalter, the commander of the I&I Russian section. Gavrisheff reported that "from all indications, Gubert is doing a swell job at Nome. His heart and soul are in his work and he really does everything possible for the Soviets. They seem to like him very much."[15]

The responsibilities of the original Russian-American Bureau of Information were also expanded. In addition to providing interpreters for air traffic control and ground service, the bureau was prepared to respond to the complaints and needs of Soviet transient air crews—ranging from billeting, messing, and transportation arrangements to filing flight clearances and encoding/decoding weather reports. Gubert assigned his liaison personnel to individual duty tours of twelve hours daily.[16]

General Jones, in addition to being commander of Nome's army garrison, was also the senior American officer there. Although not directly involved in the conduct of ALSIB route ferry operations, he greeted the arriving Soviet airmen with a warm display of cordiality. The Soviets seemed to sense the genuineness of his feelings and reacted accordingly. Jones was the genial host who entertained them and listened, through an interpreter, to the Soviet's numerous and often lengthy war stories.[17] His hospitality became legend. He was already well-known to visiting Soviet officials even before they landed at Nome. Many senior officials and flyers, especially Colonel Vasin, soon regarded Jones as a genuine American friend, and said so.

With patience, Gubert's liaison team reached a favorable relationship with the majority of the Soviets, both resident and visitor. After the Eleventh Air Force abandoned Marks Field to the ATC, American interservice bickering created a situation that, although unrelated to the liaison program, cast a shadow on Gubert's activities. Both the garrison commander and the ATC base commander had various responsibilities for constructing and maintaining the ALSIB route ground facilities for the Soviets at Nome. Interservice jurisdictional arguments over construction and supply were inevitable. Gubert struggled to keep himself aloof from the Army-ATC friction so that his energies and those of his interpreters would go to the support of the day-by-day ALSIB route operations.[18]

Since the thawing Soviet-American relationship began to revolve around General Jones and since Gubert and his men provided the language link between Jones and the Soviets, Gubert was aware that the ATC base officials believed him to be in the Jones camp. The stigma was one that Gubert from the beginning sought to avoid. He never completely succeeded in convincing the ATC officials of his impartiality.

When the first Soviet pilots began transition training at Ladd Field, ATC instructors reported that these pilots "seemed agreeable and grasped the transition instruction, but when left to themselves they reverted to obsolete and incorrect methods, such as opening the throttle to the limit soon after starting, causing the oil system to blow out."[19]

Americans rolled their eyes in dismay after the early ALSIB route flights began. Then and thereafter, Soviet pilots usually failed to make many of the final preflight inspections of instrument readings and engine performance that American pilots habitually practiced. Instead, the Soviet flyers started their engines, taxied to the point of takeoff, and promptly cleared the runway. The pilots' reliance on their engineers for aircraft mechanical perfection may have accounted for their apparent disregard for the need to verify their airplanes' readiness.

At the Fairbanks transfer point, Colonel Kiselev's engineers and mechanics minutely inspected every Lend-Lease airplane to insure that it would be prepared for immediate use on arrival at the war front. Any mechanical problem that could not be quickly solved at Ladd Field was cause for the plane to be rejected until arrangements were made to have the flaw mended.[20]

At first, ATC officials often viewed Soviet demands and complaints about the condition of some aircraft as unreasonable. They felt that nit-picking Soviet mechanics were constantly looking for problems that did not exist, thereby creating a perpetual state of apprehension or annoyance among the ATC service personnel. Colonel Kiselev knew, however, that few if any trained Soviet technicians were located on the ALSIB route beyond Nome. Once the aircraft departed from Alaskan air space for the long flight across Siberia, there was no satisfactory way to correct any problems overlooked at Ladd Field. Any mechanical oversight at Ladd Field was punishable, even though the mechanic's error may have been an honest one. Under such pressure, Soviet technical personnel were determined to locate malfunctions and equipment flaws, no matter how minor.

To the Soviets, time was a precious element when they flew airplanes from Alaska. Their compulsion for telescoping time seemed to permeate Soviet thought and action beyond American understanding. Whether adherence to this policy was responsible for any of the seventy-three Lend-Lease aircraft losses on the ALSIB route has remained an unanswered question.[21] But considering the 3,500-mile length of the ALSIB route, the loss of nine-tenths of one percent was not unreasonable. By comparison, the loss rate on the shorter 1,900-mile Northwest route was seven-tenths of one percent.

At least 140 Soviet airmen died on the ALSIB route between Fairbanks and Krasnoyarsk.[22] On the Alaskan leg of the route, a major cause of death was pilot disorientation in freakish weather conditions, resulting in midair collisions and crashes. Thirteen bodies of those who died in Alaska were originally buried in Nome's Post Cemetery No. 2 and then later reburied in the Fort Richardson National Cemetery near Anchorage.[23] Other Soviet bodies, however, may have been flown from Alaska to be buried in Soviet soil. The nearest Soviet military cemetery was at Uel'kal.

Even while Soviet-American relationships at Fairbanks remained official and proper, friction occasionally occurred. One of the earliest and most persistent sources of friction grew from the Soviets' complaint regarding the meager flow of Lend-Lease aircraft during the winter of 1942–43. That complaint was tempered somewhat when the number of delivered aircraft dramatically increased beginning in April.[24]

In June, the last month of the Second Protocol period, a record total of 329 airplanes was transferred to the Soviets.[25] When the Third Protocol went into effect in July, a similar or greater number was expected to arrive each month. Colonel Machin was delighted. The Soviet Military Mission's ferrying mechanism began to hum as flight after flight was scheduled when weather permitted. Because of the large number of aircraft involved and the continuous hours of summertime daylight, the 1st Regiment's pilots were not idle as long as Lend-Lease planes continued to pour into Ladd Field. Improvements to the Siberian bases being ahead of schedule (chap. 7), Colonel Machin was no longer concerned that the ALSIB route might not be ready for the increase in traffic. Instead, he was concerned as to whether his present body of ALSIB pilots could handle any unexpected surge in the ferrying load. Not knowing what the peak volume of aircraft might be in the future, he requested reinforcements so that he could send as many as six hundred airplanes per month over the ALSIB route. His precautions proved to be unnecessary.[26]

Each Siberian-bound flight was composed of a group of bombers or a group of fighters led by a bomber whose pilot was familiar with the route to Uel'kal. Every flight was planned as precisely as possible to ensure that the ferry pilots, after having delivered their planes to Uel'kal, were promptly returned to Ladd Field for another mission. Unpredictable weather was the major culprit when a flight's scheduled departure from Ladd Field was interrupted, delayed, or canceled.

A near-fatal accident occurred on July 2 in the midst of the ferrying flurry when a flight of ten A-20 bombers was readied at Ladd Field to leave for Nome. The flight waited for weather clearance. Clouds blocked the route west of Fairbanks, and the bombers remained grounded until their B-25 bomber pilot completed a weather reconnaissance. Having found a break in the cloud mass, the B-25 returned to Ladd Field where the A-20s were now cleared for takeoff. One of the A-20s carried two

Soviet airmen, a pilot and a navigator, Lt. Constantine P. Demyanenko. Normally, the navigator occupied the space in the bomber's nose section. The A-20s in this particular flight, however, were modified so that the navigator's space was filled with automatic weapons, and the navigator's position was moved to the second cockpit, behind the pilot's. Individual canopies covered each of the cockpits.

With the B-25 bomber leading, the flight of A-20s soared westward under the clouds, which later began to drop. Visual contact between the bombers became impossible, and the danger of midair collision was real. At the same time, Nome reported that fog had closed its field. Fortunately, one by one, the pilots of all eleven aircraft were able to make emergency landings at nearby Galena. All of the Soviet airmen were accounted for—except for the navigator Demyanenko. He had vanished.[27]

Notified of the Soviet airman's disappearance, Colonel Machin flew immediately to Galena. Together with Demyanenko's pilot, Machin inspected the A-20 for clues. The pilot remembered that he had felt an unusual "bump" when he was probing the rough air to find a way to reach Galena. Machin noted that the navigator's canopy was open. He also noted that there was a dent in the bomber's tail stabilizer. It became apparent that Demyanenko had not fastened his seat belt. Machin correctly surmised that when Demyanenko opened his canopy for better vision in the clouds, the bomber lurched, and being unsecured in his seat, the navigator was flung from the cockpit. His boots struck the tail stabilizer, but he was saved when his backpack parachute automatically opened.[28]

Machin and the ATC's search and rescue squadron concentrated their individual searches on the wilderness area northeast of Galena above the Yukon River. The likelihood that Demyanenko had survived seemed dim.

Then hope revived. A low-flying search plane sighted a piece of cloth, believed to be parachute fabric, tied to a tree. Lt. Bassell Blakesmith, piloting a float plane, returned to the earmarked area. Accompanied by his ATC search and rescue squadron commander, Maj. R. C. Ragle, Blakesmith passed over the area at low level and located Demyanenko standing in a clearing and waving wildly. Blakesmith landed his plane on the nearest available lake and evacuated Demyanenko, who was covered with bites from hordes of flying insects. After recovering from his ordeal at the Ladd Field station hospital, Demyanenko returned to his ferrying duties on the ALSIB route. In 1944, promoted to captain, he was transferred to combat duty on the war front.[29]

For his rescue, Blakesmith was given two awards. One was from the

Soviets—the Order of the Red Star—and the other from ATC's Alaskan Wing—the Air Medal.[30]

The Soviets in Alaska were permitted to move freely on the bases at Fairbanks and Nome. The only restricted areas were those where American aircraft were parked. Maj. Gen. John R. Deane, the commander of the U.S. Military Mission to Moscow, traveled between Moscow and Washington via the ALSIB route. During a Fairbanks stopover, he reported that he was amazed by the contrast between the way that Americans were treated in Moscow and the circumstances of the Soviets in Alaska.[31] At least half of Ladd Field, he said, was under Soviet control. Barracks, offices, hangars, and shops were released to the Soviets. American and Soviet officers ate the same food at a central mess. And most notable of all, the Soviets were welcomed to the base facilities, including access to the base exchange and motor vehicles.

The base exchanges at Ladd Field and Marks Field were supplied with ordinary goods unavailable in the war-ravaged Soviet Union. The appealing merchandise in the shops of Fairbanks and Nome also beckoned. Stocked with American currency, the eager Soviets bought candy, soap, perfume, cosmetics, lingerie, women's shoes, and even canned goods. These items were boxed and stuffed into Soviet transports bound for Siberia. With the boxes went the hope that they somehow would reach the hands of relatives.[32]

When Soviet officers required transportation to Fairbanks, the Ladd Field motor pool dispatched sedans with American army drivers to deliver them to designated points. The vehicles and drivers later returned the officers to Ladd Field. A similar courtesy was available to Soviet officers at Nome.

All in all, despite some misunderstandings and lingering concerns, both Soviets and Americans entered the midsummer season of 1943 in a more relaxed mood. The ATC's Alaskan Wing was in the midst of reorganization and visible improvements in ATC's delivery capability could be seen in the increased numbers of airplanes landing at Fairbanks. The Soviets' complaints decreased proportionately.

Then, on July 15, at the moment when the welcome flurry of ferry activity diverted Soviet-American attention from their differences to their common endeavors, an unexpected crisis began to develop. It quickly clouded the international atmosphere at Fairbanks, curbing Soviet enthusiasm and arousing fresh American doubts.

At the center of the crisis were two of the NKVD officers responsible for intelligence and security control measures in the Soviet Military

Mission: Capt. Dimitri M. Vologov, the mission's senior intelligence officer, and Lt. Makary F. Komar, its cryptographer.[33]

On the fateful July 15, Vologov and Komar went to the Ladd Field motor pool to engage a vehicle and driver. Pvt. John O. White had been a Fairbanks taxi driver before his induction into military service. Stationed at Ladd Field, he was assigned to motor pool duty. He apparently was a driver favored by various Soviet officials, and White told his associates that the Soviets were generous with their gratuities. On this memorable occasion, he was the driver for Vologov and Komar, who knew him well enough to call him "Johnny."

Indicating that they wanted to pick wild flowers, Vologov directed White to drive them about five miles northwest of Fairbanks along the Farmers Loop Road leading to a small body of water known as Blaine's (or "Ballaine") Lake. Nearby was a smaller lake, and the University of Alaska's campus was located only a mile away. The two lakes were popular with Soviet officials, who were known to use the area for picnicking and swimming.

During the trip from Ladd Field, Vologov sat in the front seat of the automobile with White to direct the driver where they wanted to go. Because of the language barrier, conversation between the Soviets and White was limited. Vologov told the American investigators that "Johnny had a little Russian-English language dictionary, so we could tell him not to slam the door and little things like that." Vologov and Komar tried to joke with White and teased him about the ring of fat around the driver's waist.

When they arrived at Blaine's Lake, the two officers, after leaving White with the parked vehicle, entered the adjacent dense woods. They later stated that they picked wild flowers and spent some time shooting at trees with a small caliber rifle. They then returned to the lake. They discovered that the car had been moved down the road and parked closer to the lake's edge.

White was nowhere to be seen. Repeated calls of "Johnny, Johnny, Johnny" by Komar and Vologov and their whistles brought no response. Komar hailed a passing automobile and asked in broken English to be taken to a telephone. He was delivered to the nearby university library. Komar, agitated and perspiring, asked the librarian, Helen Wilcox, to telephone the "Russian Department at Ladd Field" for him. He talked with Michael E. Kharitonov, the auditor of the Soviet Purchasing Commission, after which, at Kharitonov's request, Komar returned the telephone to Mrs. Wilcox. Kharitonov then explained to her that Komar "was afraid that their driver had been drowned in a small lake nearby," and that help was being sent. Four American soldiers, later joined by two more, arrived and began a search of the area. They first found a pile of clothing at the edge of Blaine's Lake. The clothing and the personal possessions in them were identified as belonging to White. Further searching of the dense woods located a heap of smoldering ashes where a considerable amount of paper had been burned. Examination of the residue revealed that the papers had been cryptographic materials.

The search continued, but White's whereabouts remained a mystery. Either White had entered the lake and drowned, as Komar had said even before he and Vologov were aware of the pile of clothing, or White had played an elaborate trick to cover a scheme to desert. Because the latter possibility could not immediately be eliminated, a general alert was issued throughout Alaska to search for White and prevent him leaving Alaska by ship or plane.

On the following day, July 16, empty small caliber shells were found near where the papers had been burned, and two ducks, killed by small caliber bullets, were discovered floating on Blaine's Lake. Ladd Field's base intelligence officer interviewed both Vologov and Komar, who admitted that he and Vologov had fired about eight bullets in the woods, but they "were shooting for nickels" only.

Soldiers in boats crisscrossed Blaine's Lake repeatedly, dragging grappling hooks. They continued to do so for three days, until July 19. Their efforts were fruitless. Then, for two days following, the lake was thoroughly and expertly dynamited in efforts to raise White's body. Nothing. In a last-ditch effort to find White's body if indeed he had drowned, the Ladd Field engineer officer was ordered to drain the lake. On July 21, a ten-inch diesel-operated pump was installed and the slow process of draining the lake began.

Meanwhile on July 19, Vologov confessed in the presence of Colonel Kiselev that he and Komar had indeed been shooting ducks on Blaine's Lake prior to their burning classified documents, having left White with the parked car. Vologov said that in their earlier interview with the base intelligence officer, they had denied the duck shooting because they knew that it was a violation of the Alaskan game laws.

Colonel Keillor, commander of Ladd Field, sent a formal memorandum to Colonel Machin on July 22: "It is respectfully requested that your office detain Capt. Dimitri M. Vologov and Lt. Makary F. Komar on Ladd Field and/or immediate vicinity of Fairbanks until the conclusion of the investigation of the whereabouts of Pvt. John White."

On July 26, eleven days after his disappearance, John White's body was found. Operating day and night, the pump had removed an estimated four million gallons of water to lower the level of the lake to less than three feet. White's remains were in remarkably good shape at the bottom of a deep hole about one hundred feet from the shoreline where his clothing had been discovered. Signs of foul play were not visible on the body.

Rumors circulated in Fairbanks, where the worst conclusion was reached, namely that for whatever reason, John White had been deliberately killed. The Soviets at Ladd Field were tight-lipped and the general atmosphere at the base was tense even as the Soviet Military Mission concentrated its attention on moving a record number of aircraft to Siberia.

There were two Komars at Ladd Field, and both were Soviet lieutenants. One was Makary F. Komar and the other was Mark I. Komar, an assistant flight leader in the 1st Bomber Squadron, regularly involved in the accelerated ferrying operations. On the arrival and departure manifests of Soviet personnel filed at Ladd Field, the names were submitted in abbreviated form: "M. Komar." Because of the heightened tension, when the name of M. Komar appeared on the manifest of Soviets scheduled to depart immediately aboard the latest flight of Lend-Lease aircraft for Siberia, Ladd Field authorities ordered the flight to be grounded.

Was Makary Komar attempting to leave Alaska for Siberian sanctuary? Investigation revealed, of course, that the Komar concerned was Mark, not Makary. Colonel Machin, very much aware of the Fairbanks rumors, was upset. He was especially distressed because the hasty grounding order revealed the heightened degree of current American suspicion, and he protested the unwarranted interruption of his ferrying schedule.

Because of the inconsistencies and omissions in the statements made by Vologov and Komar on July 16, the U.S. investigators requested the base intelligence officer to arrange for a second interview with the two Soviet officers in order to establish a complete and accurate record of what had actually happened on July 15. For reasons never explained, the Ladd Field commander, Colonel Keillor, denied the request, thereby shutting down any further investigative probing.

Two American military surgeons performed an autopsy on John White's body. They concurred in their findings: "Subject's death was caused by drowning. Careful examination revealed no indication of violence to the body, other than the slight bleeding from nostrils and ears caused by the use of heavy charges of dynamite in Blaine's Lake in an effort to cause the body to surface during the earlier attempts in the search." The official investigation therefore concluded that "John White entered Blaine's Lake for an unknown purpose on 15 July and drowned therein."[34]

White's mother and stepfather were convinced, however, that their son had been murdered.[35] They said he could not swim and was afraid of water. John White was buried at Fairbanks on July 29.

A noticeable cooling of the Soviet-American relationship at Fairbanks was expected regardless of the outcome of the investigation. The damage could not be ignored. But the relationship did not appear to be permanently impaired. Since Ladd Field officials did not make specific charges against Vologov or Komar, the Soviet Military Mission could logically conclude that neither officer was persona non grata. Nor was either recalled to the Soviet Union. Both continued to perform their functions and exercise their authority within the Soviet Military Mission.

During July, the ATC and the Soviet Military Mission did not allow the tensions and suspicions generated by the disappearance of John White to cause any extended interruption in the momentum of delivering aircraft to and through Alaska. A total of 320 airplanes was transferred during the month.[36] This peak number was not again attained for another year.

In the first week of August, 1943, adverse weather conditions beyond the Bering Sea caused the eastern-most ALSIB route bases at Uel'kal and Markovo to be closed temporarily. Since new Lend-Lease aircraft continued to arrive at Ladd Field, Colonel Machin likewise continued to relay the aircraft westward to Nome. With the arrival of flight after flight, a total of 132 airplanes soon were parked at Nome before ferrying operations could be resumed.[37] Peter Gamov, commander of the 1st Bomber Squadron, was one of the busy pilots involved in the scheduled ferrying activity. On August 4, he had another opportunity to demonstrate his skill and daring as a pilot.[38]

In his role as the designated "leader of fighters," Gamov departed Ladd Field in his B-25 bomber, collected his assigned group of P-39 fighters, and headed for Nome. Soon, however, Gamov's crew mechanic reported to him that "something was wrong with the bomber's nosewheel." Releasing control of the bomber to his copilot, Gamov examined the situation. He saw that a strut that should have been holding the wheel in position was loose and the wheel itself was dangling. Landing would be extremely dangerous because use of the bomber's brakes could cause the airplane to ground-loop.

Gamov by radio ordered the flight of fighters to continue to and land at Galena. And wait. Turning back to Ladd Field, he reported his problem. Colonel Machin rushed to the control tower, as did Elena Makarova. (Prior to takeoff, Gamov had proposed marriage to Makarova. In the control tower, she now realized how great was the danger that Gamov was facing and decided forthwith to marry him if he survived this latest gamble.) Machin ordered Gamov to belly-land the bomber after the Ladd Field ambulances and fire-fighting trucks were in place along the runway.

Gamov recalled that Lt. Nicholas de Tolly, who had been his ATC transition flight instructor, had told him about a similar emergency situation. According to de Tolly, an American bomber with a broken front wheel had landed safely by using the following procedure: while the bomber was landing on the runway, two men in the beds of two trucks racing on either side of the plane passed a rope across the tail to hold it down when the plane was braked to a stop.

Gamov wanted to try the experiment. Machin was reluctant to do so because a Soviet plane with defective brakes had recently plunged into the Tanana River at the end of the Ladd Field runway.

Machin was persuaded to agree. He began giving Gamov instructions concerning when and where to land. Two trucks were speeding in place when Gamov landed, but his bomber ran freely for half the length of the runway before the trucks caught up and snared the tail with rope. Slowly the plane and truck brakes were applied in time to bring the bomber to a halt at the edge of the river.

With the exception of Gamov, the bomber crew members and an American passenger were seated as far to the rear interior of the bomber as possible, and their combined weight was enough to prevent the bomber's tipping forward. However, no matter how much Machin shouted into his microphone for the crew to sit still, the excited men immediately ran forward to the exit ladder. A hangar crew bringing aircraft nose supports arrived too late. The nose-heavy bomber tipped and damaged its propellers.

7.
Aircraft Quantity and Quality

Soviet military historians now concede that the extent of American Lend-Lease assistance to the Soviet Union during the war was considerable. In their view, the Lend-Lease program had many positive aspects, one of which was the delivery of aircraft via the ALSIB route.[1]

The Red Air Force was nearly destroyed in the first months of the war with Germany. The Soviet aircraft industry, however, was able to relocate many of its factories and production allowed the air force to contest the German pressure on the retreating Red Army. As the Red Air Force was reconstituted and expanded, Lend-Lease resources also reinforced it throughout the war. The more than fourteen thousand Lend-Lease aircraft made a significant, if not decisive, contribution to the Soviet war effort.[2]

About 12 percent of Red Air Force strength was provided by American-made aircraft.[3] Over half of the U.S. Lend-Lease airplanes, or about 7 percent of Red Air Force strength, was delivered via the ALSIB route.[4]

From the beginning, the Soviet Military Mission in Alaska remained constantly concerned with the quantity and quality of the Lend-Lease aircraft. By the time the ALSIB route completed its first year of operation in 1943, the quantity was rising and the quality of the P-40 and P-39 fighters, the A-20 and B-25 bombers, and the C-47 transport was tested.

Forty-eight P-40 fighters, made famous by the Flying Tigers volunteers in China, were among the first of the Lend-Lease aircraft made available to the Soviets at Fairbanks in 1942. Chronic generator problems and shortages of essential spare parts were among the difficulties that the Soviet pilots encountered. Another two thousand were delivered by other routes but no further P-40s were ferried via the ALSIB route.[5]

A year after the opening of the ferry route, three P-47 fighters were flown to Fairbanks and transferred to the Soviets. The new high-altitude fighters had been ordered by the Red Air Force for testing in combat. Although some were delivered by other routes to fulfill Third Protocol commitments, no additional P-47s traversed the ALSIB route.[6]

The P-39 Airacobra, despite its initial problems with piston rings and spark plugs, soon became a favorite not only with the Soviet inspectors and mechanics in Alaska but with Red Air Force combat pilots as well.[7] Called variously the *kobry* or *kobryshka* ("dear little cobra"), the nimble airplane attained major victories over German foes. Powerfully armed with a 37-mm cannon, the P-39 was also reported to be highly successful in sweeping attacks against ground targets.[8] At the request of Soviet officials, minor changes were made at Ladd Field in some of the P-39 cockpits, apparently for the convenience and comfort of women pilots who were reported to be ferrying the planes in Siberia.[9]

The B-25 bomber also had the full approval of inspectors, mechanics, and pilots as being thoroughly reliable. It was destined to be used extensively on night missions against enemy railheads, artillery, and troop concentrations.[10]

In addition to the steady flow of standard B-25 models as required by protocol commitments, an experimental model arrived at Ladd Field in 1943 with a recoilless 75-mm gun mounted in it. The Soviets, curious about the innovation, referred to it as "flying field artillery." The B-25, scheduled for testing in the Soviet Union, carried a supply of special test rounds. According to reports from Uel'kal after the bomber arrived there, Colonel Mazuruk, commander of the ALSIB route operations, personally test-fired the gun while the B-25 was on the ground there, and Mazuruk "seemed well pleased with the flying artillery's performance."[11]

As the experimental bomber crossed Siberia, senior officials at each base and refueling stop also succumbed to curiosity and test-fired the gun. By the time that the B-25 reached an official Soviet testing ground, the supply of special rounds was exhausted. No further copies of the experimental model appeared at Ladd Field.[12]

A-20 bombers were the first Lend-Lease craft to traverse the virgin ALSIB route from Alaska in 1942, but the Soviets were not especially impressed with them. Although fast and agile, the A-20 was vulnerable because it was lightly armored and machine guns provided its only defense. In addition, pilots worried because the bomber required longer than normal runways for taking off. Since the new bases along the ALSIB route were still in the process of improving and lengthening their runways, A-20 ferry pilots kept their fingers crossed each time they opened their throttles to go aloft.

By spring of 1943, the new A-20G model was modified to add some armor and four 20-mm cannons that could be mounted in the plane's nose. Even so, the Soviets considered the A-20 to have inadequate armor protection and to be vulnerable to attack from the sides and rear. Nonetheless, the A-20's heavy firepower, high speed, and maneuverability earned it the reputation of being a versatile night fighter, attack plane, or light bomber.[13]

Col. Pavel Nedosekin was a recognized innovator in the use of air combat teams combining bombers with fighters. As acting commander of the mobilizing 1st Ferrying Aviation Regiment in 1942, Nedosekin had led the inaugural flight of Lend-Lease aircraft from Fairbanks to Nome. After being returned to combat duty in 1943, he commanded a mixed aviation regiment that was commended for its role in the Red Army's Smolensk offensive. Nedosekin's regiment had five assigned squadrons of Lend-Lease aircraft—two of A-20 bombers and three of P-39 fighters.[14]

The slow-speed C-47 transport was considered thoroughly reliable and was used to haul personnel and cargo both to and within the battlefields. The Soviets obtained hundreds through Lend-Lease arrangements and all were delivered via the ALSIB route. Operation of the ferry route across Alaska, Siberia, and beyond also depended on the transports for movement of essential supplies and personnel. Every foot of cargo space was precious. The Soviet Military Mission was ordered not to allow a transport to leave Alaska for Siberia until it was loaded to its capacity.[15]

During the severe winter of 1942–43, American civilian contract mechanics based at Ladd Field made modifications in order to heat some of the C-47s. They cut stovepipe holes in the top of the fuselages and installed coal-burning stoves.[16] A few of the Lend-Lease C-47s that operated in Siberia were also fitted that way.[17]

In addition to using the C-47s for transport purposes, the Red Air Force converted some of them into bombers. The C-47 "bomber" carried its load of explosives in racks under the wings. It was armed with two heavy machine guns installed in a rotating turret above the center of the fuselage, two light machine guns on each side of the fuselage pointed to the rear, and two light machine guns fixed in the nose so that the pilot could fire them.[18]

Despite the hardships endured during the 1942–43 winter, the ALSIB route bases in Siberia continued to be improved at a steady rate. Some had been hastily scratched from the Siberian wilderness in 1942, but a year later they were regularly receiving and servicing Lend-Lease aircraft from Alaska and sending them on their way westward. When interruptions in the ferry service occurred, the bases' personnel and makeshift facilities were rarely at fault. Interruptions were usually caused either by weather conditions or natural disasters, over which Soviet personnel obviously had no control, or by slowdowns or stoppages in the flow of Lend-Lease aircraft, for which the Soviets blamed the Americans.

At Uel'kal, the first major base in Siberia, the corduroy runways of timber proved to be quite satisfactory. Unlike runways made of concrete or asphalt, the wooden runways required little maintenance. The availability of lumber from the limitless forests made this type of runway a pattern for similar landing strips in the interior of Siberia. Uel'kal's main runway and the parallel auxiliary one were reported by the pilots to be longer and wider than those at Nome.[19] The introduction of runway lights was completed in anticipation of increased ferry activity during the approaching 1943–44 winter months.[20] A radio beam was being installed to give direction to incoming pilots. To enhance the base's operation, forty-three women were assigned to administrative and communications duties.[21]

Markovo's flight operations were interrupted in early summer by a one-time shortage of fuel supplies and by dense smoke from nearby massive forest fires. Operations soon returned to normal.[22] The Markovo base was used as an intermediate refueling point for P-39 fighters before they resumed the long nonstop flight to Seymchan. No other landing strips existed between Markovo and Seymchan (chap. 8), but in emergencies, some of the scant roadways were available in summer and frozen lakes in winter.[23] The Markovo and Seymchan bases each got an additional runway and new buildings.[24]

Also in anticipation of increased traffic, construction of a second air base at Yakutsk was nearing completion,[25] and three radio control points were installed between Uel'kal and Yakutsk to make the route less hazardous.[26]

Krasnoyarsk, the western terminal of the ALSIB route, became the principal technical base where each of the arriving Lend-Lease airplanes underwent an immediate mandatory twenty-five-hour inspection to determine its condition. Following the inspection, a waiting air crew was assigned to it. As sufficient P-39, A-20, and B-25 planes were declared technically fit, crews were formed into squadrons and trained at Krasnoyarsk before being sent westward for combat duty.[27]

At the end of the first week in August, 1943, weather conditions in eastern Siberia that had closed the bases at Uel'kal and Markovo improved enough to permit resumption of ferrying. The week's backlog of 132 aircraft parked at Nome began to dwindle as pilots repeatedly crossed the Bering Sea to waiting bases.[28]

On August 11, Colonel Machin took advantage of the improved weather. He boarded a C-47 transport at Ladd Field and flew nonstop to Uel'kal. The colonel had been among the first of the high-ranking Soviet officials assigned to Alaskan duty, and his flight to Siberia marked his first departure from Alaska since his arrival a year earlier. He habitually had piloted his own plane during his frequent visits to Nome, but on this occasion he was a passenger.[29]

Days passed and Machin did not return to Alaska. According to rumor, he was en route to Moscow. In his absence, command of the Soviet Military Mission was passed to Machin's executive officer, Colonel Kiselev, chief of engineering and inspection services.

When the surge of Lend-Lease deliveries began during the summer months, the two airfields at Nome were filling to capacity. Igor Gubert recalled that "when we had daylight around the clock, flights of airplanes came in all the time. I had only three interpreters for the line. I was dashing between the two fields because I had to control those planes from the tower until Vasin [Colonel Vasin, commander of the 1st Ferrying Aviation Regiment] landed and came to the tower to relieve me."[30]

Gubert confessed that air traffic control under such circumstances was especially nerve-wracking. There were major crises when unexpected low fog suddenly blanketed the fields and aircraft arrived above the fog with insufficient fuel to take them to the nearest emergency field.

"I remember a case," Gubert said, "when low fog swept from the Bering Sea and covered the air fields like a vast white sheet. Soviet planes were buzzing above the fog like swarms of bees with no place to land. I sent two of my men to stand at either side of the main runway where they shot flares through the fog every thirty seconds. I was in the control tower directing the pilots to fly between the two flares visible above the fog." Guided by the flares, the pilots penetrated the fog blanket and found the runway for a safe landing.

Gubert knew that if a Soviet plane had an accident while landing under his direction, he would not be able to shift the blame regardless of the circumstances. Once, when fog was a problem to incoming aircraft, Colonel Vasin fortunately had already landed and relieved Gubert in the control tower. Within minutes, Maj. Nicholas Senchenko, assistant commander of the 1st Fighter Squadron, landed under Vasin's direction and drove his P-39 fighter into a gravel pit beside the runway. Gubert was thankful for Vasin's timely presence.

Within the Soviet ranks at Nome, Gubert attracted one natural, powerful opponent, a man identified by Gubert as being the Soviet Military Mission's third NKVD officer.

Capt. Michael M. Gubin, an English-speaking officer, came from Ladd Field on special assignment to Nome during the first week of August. At Ladd Field he was on Colonel Kiselev's staff, where he was engaged in engineering and intelligence activities. During his short visit to Nome, Gubin managed to arouse the suspicions of some of the Soviet mechanics because he failed to demonstrate any special knowledge of aircraft engineering.

A month later, on September 4, Gubin again came to Nome, this time on permanent assignment. As Colonel Kiselev's engineering representative, he was in charge of Nome's mechanics. He also was involved in intelligence activities.

The designated senior Soviet officer at Nome was an aviator who held the dual post of officer-in-charge of the Soviet installation and navigator for the 1st Ferrying Aviation Regiment. A series of aviators, some of whom were junior to Gubin, were rotated through the commander/navigator position. Gubin unsuccessfully challenged each of them for the apparent purpose of getting control of the Nome installation. He became a major irritant to the Soviet flying personnel, who did not try to conceal their dislike. In some instances, senior Soviet officers passing through Nome were overheard to refer to Gubin as "that NKVD son of a bitch."[31]

Despite his knowledge of English, Gubin did not mix with the Americans and avoided contact with General Jones and his staff. From the time of Gubin's arrival, the relationship between him and Gubert was strained. "Our meetings were always short and to the point," Gubert recalled. "I could not avoid his animosity."

Igor Gubert remembered vividly when he encountered Gubin in the base gymnasium. Outfitted with boxing gloves, Gubert was hammering a heavy punching bag when Gubin arrived. "Not saying much, Gubin took off his shirt and put on gloves," Gubert said, "and [without warn-

ing] we were fighting! After a few minutes, somebody summoned a senior Soviet officer who stopped the fight. I don't remember who he was,
but I do clearly remember that it was I, not Gubin, that got the cheers
from the Soviet onlookers. I also noticed that my relationship with Gubin
seemed to improve a bit after the fight."[32]

Igor Gubert described an incident that occurred when he was taking
two Soviet flying officers and three of Gubin's mechanics on a fishing
excursion. "All six of us were in a military truck," Gubert said. "One of
Gubin's men was drunk and misbehaved in words and gestures toward
one of the officers. Enraged, the officer reacted immediately by reaching for his pistol. Fortunately, he did not have it with him. Then he
reached for the other officer's pistol, saying that he would shoot that
son of a bitch. During the struggle that followed, Gubin's other two men
grabbed the drunken mechanic and tossed him from the back of the moving truck onto the road." Igor Gubert explained to the angry officer that
unless he wanted to cause a great deal of trouble for General Jones, any
shooting of Soviet mechanics should be done only on Soviet soil. Calm-
ing himself, the officer agreed. He asked Gubert not to report what had
happened.[33]

Excessive drinking became a serious Soviet problem at Nome, so much
so that one flying officer was grounded, and similar action was threatened for others. In late August, the Soviet commander issued orders pro-
hibiting Soviet personnel from bringing liquor from Nome to the base.
Individuals later were required to obtain a special pass to go to Nome
where they were ordered not to drink. In December, several Soviet
officers at Nome were again reprimanded for intoxication.[34]

The quantity of Lend-Lease aircraft on the ALSIB route destined for the
Krasnoyarsk terminal was easier for the Soviets to monitor than their
quality. Fluctuations in the flow of aircraft immediately caught Soviet
attention. Even the weather-related interruption of deliveries from Alaska
in early August triggered a Soviet investigation.

Lt. Gen. A. A. Avseyevich arrived in Nome on September 8. As chief
of Soviet airborne ferrying activities on all delivery routes, including
ALSIB, he had orders from Stalin to inspect the ALSIB route on both sides
of the Bering Sea and to investigate and report on the relationship between the Soviets and Americans in Alaska. During his overnight Nome
visit, Avseyevich gave explicit orders to the Soviet personnel: "The planes
must go through to Siberia despite the weather. They must go! The planes
are most important." As a result, three flights soon departed Nome for

Uel'kal in weather that ordinarily grounded the aircraft under the standing policy in force prior to the general's arrival.[35]

Avseyevich continued his trip on September 9 to Fairbanks, where he remained for ten days before retracing his route to Moscow. On the eve of his September 18 departure, he decorated twenty officers of the Soviet Military Mission at a banquet held at Ladd Field. Sixteen of the decorated men were assigned to the 1st Ferrying Aviation Regiment, and the other four were engineering and supervisory officers.

In his banquet speech, Avseyevich assured his Soviet audience that Stalin made frequent inquiries about the condition of and successes on the ALSIB route and particularly about the situation at Ladd Field. Stalin was interested in every detail of "the Russian colony in Alaska," he said.[36]

Following Avseyevich's departure for Moscow to make his report, General Belyaev, chairman of the Soviet Purchasing Commission and coordinator of Lend-Lease affairs in Washington, arrived in Fairbanks on September 27, also bound for Moscow. Belyaev, who had been a major figure in the negotiations that led to the opening of the ALSIB route in 1942, was now traveling it for the first time. He praised the manner in which the route had blossomed during its first year of life. He appeared to be openly impressed by the urgency with which Soviet-American coordination effected the transfer and movement of aircraft destined for the German front.[37] Belyaev traveled the route in one direction only. He did not return to his post in Washington (chap. 8).

To Alaskans, as the first anniversary of the opening of the ALSIB route neared, the existence of the Lend-Lease ferrying activities was an annoying official secret. The presence of Soviet personnel at and between Fairbanks and Nome was no longer a curiosity in the communities where identified Soviet aircraft, flight after flight, came and went. Candid Soviet officials admitted that Japanese cultural and commercial agents posted in major Siberian cities were not blind to the masses of Lend-Lease aircraft passing through Siberia from Alaska. American media correspondents were exasperated by the rigid censorship that blocked their reporting of Alaska's role in the war, including the story of Soviet-American cooperation against a common enemy, Germany.[38]

After the Japanese seizure of Attu and Kiska islands in June, 1942, public interest in the Alaskan military situation had been dampened by censorship, but congressional interest had not. Spurred by the Japanese threat, a congressional delegation headed by Senator Albert ("Happy") Chandler of Kentucky arrived in Alaska two months later for discussions with the military commanders. At that time, members of the delegation briefly visited Fairbanks and Nome.

A year later, in late August, 1943, another delegation also visited Fairbanks while Colonel Machin was absent, presumably in Moscow. Included in the delegation was Senator William Langer of North Dakota. According to Drew Pearson's nationally syndicated "Washington Merry-Go-Round" column released on September 16, 1943, Senator Langer was interested in the shipment of aircraft to the Soviet Union via Fairbanks:

> It is no longer a military secret that U.S. planes are being delivered by this Siberian Great Circle route, and Senator Langer dropped in for a chat with two Russians who were piloting planes across the Bering Strait.
>
> One was Col. P. S. Kiselev, chief of the Russian military mission in Fairbanks; the other, Technical Sergeant Inspector George A. Timofiev. Both expressed indignation that the United States had not lived up to its agreement regarding plane deliveries. . . . The Russians felt that the United States should live up to their promises or not promise at all.[39]

Drew Pearson's column appeared at a time when the tensions created by the John White drowning were easing. The remarks attributed to Senator Langer had a renewed disquieting effect on the delicate Soviet-American sense of mutual trust. An American investigation concluded that Drew Pearson had erred: neither man with whom Langer had engaged in casual conversation was a pilot. Colonel Kiselev, of course, was not the chief of the Soviet mission, although he was the senior officer present during the absence of Colonel Machin. And the sergeant was not a Soviet at all, but rather Sgt. George de Timofeyev, an American I&I interpreter. Both Kiselev and de Timofeyev vehemently denied that the senator had been told that the Soviet Union was dissatisfied with the aircraft deliveries.[40]

The damage was done, however, never to be completely repaired. "Colonel Kiselev must have been reprimanded to the edge of Siberia," one I&I liaison officer said. For the remainder of the year, the mere mention of an American journalist or senator would turn the outwardly mild-mannered Soviet officer into an openly hostile one. Once Kiselev even threatened to destroy the camera that an American photographer was attempting to focus on a group of Soviet airmen.[41]

Another development making the Soviet presence in Alaska even more public occurred in late September, 1943. Alaska Defense Command officials learned that the Soviet government had arranged with the State Department for Soviet wives and children to join their husbands and fathers at Fairbanks and Nome. The arrangement applied only to officers who were permanently stationed in Alaska. Fourteen wives and children were already en route. Additional visas were being sought so that families of other Soviet officers could also come to Alaska, on the grounds that they were "dependents of government officials."[42]

The only Soviet spouse already in Alaska was Dina V. Anisimova, who had arrived with the original Soviet cadres in 1942. Her husband was Alexis A. Anisimov, now in charge of the Soviet Purchasing Commission's office at Fairbanks. Dina Anisimova was employed as the commission's secretary. Two other civilians, Evgeniya F. Mazur and her son Anatoly, aged fifteen, although without a visible official sponsor, were employed by the commission as typist and office boy.

After a seven-week absence, Colonel Machin returned from Moscow to Nome, arriving on October 1.[43] With him were his wife, Lydia A. Machina, and their two sons, aged eight and four; Maria P. Kiseleva, wife of Colonel Kiselev; Nina S. Kalinnikova, wife of Major Kalinnikov, and their six-year-old son; Valentina Strizhkova, wife of Lieutenant Colonel Strizhkov, and their son of four; and each with two children seven or younger, Elena D. Yatzkevich, wife of Major Yatzkevich, and Galena I. Gubina, wife of Captain Gubin (appendix B).

The Soviet group spent the night at Nome, where Colonel Machin discussed his trip with General Jones. He told Jones that the performance of Lend-Lease aircraft on the war front was reported to be "most satisfactory." Machin also invited Jones to come to Fairbanks as a guest of the Soviet Military Mission later in October to celebrate the first anniversary of the ALSIB route's inauguration, assuring the general that a Soviet transport would be made available to fly Jones and his party to Ladd Field and back.

The following day, Colonel Machin and the group of Soviet dependents, except Captain Gubin's family, flew to Fairbanks. A search for available housing having produced no results, the families moved temporarily into the Pioneer Hotel. Because of the housing shortage, any Soviet plans for bringing additional families were suspended. A major influx of Soviet dependents in the immediate future appeared unlikely.[44]

Following the example set by Dina Anisimova in the Soviet Purchasing Commission office, Maria Kiseleva became the secretary of the Soviet Military Mission.

The dependents' trip across Siberia to "the Russian colony in Alaska" had been long and tiring. Because of fatigue, the early stages of three-year-old Ludmila Yatzkevich's illness were not seriously regarded, on the assumption that her health would improve with rest. Major and Elena Yatzkevich's daughter later was rushed to the Ladd Field station hospital. Her parents waited helplessly as the child suffocated from the effects of diptheria on October 15, only two weeks after arriving in Alaska.[45]

Soviet officials reminded their American counterparts that the deficit of more than three hundred planes from the Second Protocol commitments was still outstanding. In view of the approaching 1943–44 winter, Soviet concern was starting to mount as regards whether the July-August-September delivery rates could be maintained at the latest level and whether the Second Protocol shortage could be whittled.[46]

Machin, having resumed command of the Soviet Military Mission, was cheered by the record of ATC's increased delivery of aircraft during his absence. Apparently feeling a need to demonstrate Soviet appreciation for the recent surge in aircraft arrivals at Ladd Field, Machin made an unexpected approach to George Kisevalter for advice. Kisevalter, as commander of the I&I Russian section, was directing the section's activities from Alaska Defense Command headquarters at Fort Richardson, from which he made frequent visits to Ladd Field. Machin's reaction to Kisevalter's visits had been cool, and Kisevalter believed that Machin suspected him of being an intelligence officer. Kisevalter, on his latest periodic visit, was therefore surprised when Machin asked for help.

Machin invited Kisevalter to come to his quarters. Both men were stiff and proper until Machin revealed the purpose of his invitation. "He asked me if he should reward the outstanding American ferry pilots for their fine performance," Kisevalter recalled. "Machin proposed a gift of three hundred dollars." Kisevalter's response was *nyet*, don't give money! He told Machin that a monetary gift had no significance except to finance an evening of gambling. Instead, Kisevalter suggested that Machin arrange to give each outstanding flyer a written commendation and a bottle of vodka.[47]

Machin accepted Kisevalter's suggestion and put it into effect. An additional important outcome of the meeting was the change in Machin's attitude toward Kisevalter. He no longer shunned Kisevalter when he later needed advice on Soviet-American problems.

His impulse to reward the feats of U.S. ferry pilots appeared to be a part of Machin's desire to allay the dampening effects of the John White and Drew Pearson controversies on Soviet-American relations at Fairbanks. Machin also was eager to fulfill his plan to celebrate the first anniversary of the Alaska-Siberian Lend-Lease connection. Accordingly, on October 14, the Soviet Military Mission commemorated the milestone by hosting a festive dinner at Ladd Field. Among the American guests were General Gaffney from his ATC wing headquarters at Edmonton and General Jones from Nome. As promised, Machin arranged for Jones and his aides to make the trip via Soviet transport.[48]

Machin's renewed presence at Fairbanks, the arrival of Soviet officers' families for residence in Alaska, and the anniversary celebration all signaled that, in the Soviet view, the ALSIB route operation was now firmly established. The barrier of Soviet suspicion had been penetrated to some degree, and the Soviets were demonstrating their appreciation for the quality and the increasing quantity of Lend-Lease aircraft.

8.
Winds
of Change

By November 1943, as the Arctic winds grew stronger, other winds of change were noted in Alaska. A new era in the aircraft shuttling operation to the German front was slowly developing.

The Alaska Defense Command was redesignated as the independent Alaskan Department. In the war with Japan, the Eleventh Air Force in the liberated Aleutian Islands launched a two-year bombing campaign of attrition against enemy military targets in the Kurile Islands.

At the same time, subtle changes were felt in the Soviet-American attitudes and behavior on the ALSIB route across Alaska. Although recurring incidents aggravated both the Soviet Military Mission and the ATC, a new show of American cooperation strengthened the delicate Soviet-American relationship: the Soviet Military Mission was permitted to use the Alaska Highway telephone service from Fairbanks so that the mission could communicate with Soviet authorities in Washington.[1]

In the weeks following the publication of Drew Pearson's newspaper column, the Soviets at Ladd Field continued to be cautious in any discussions concerning the war, aircraft ferrying operations, or conditions in Siberia. However, their attitudes seemed to grow less tense than in the immediate wake of the publicity generated by Pearson.[2]

Alaskans had scarcely been blind to the presence of Soviet flyers and airplanes since September, 1942. The War Department now faced the realization that the rationale for concealing the existence of the Lend-Lease route no longer had validity. On November 23, two months after Pearson's column was released, the War Department publicly confirmed that Lend-Lease aircraft were being delivered to Soviet pilots at Fairbanks.[3]

Newspaper editors, immediately reacting to the announcement, assumed that they were freed of censorship controls regarding the ALSIB route. Censorship authorities were quick to respond negatively. Details of the ferry route's operations were still considered to be classified. Earlier regulations to control the release of military information concerning the Soviet-American activity remained virtually unchanged.[4] Media outlets were requested to cooperate.

As the swirl of comings and goings increased at Ladd Field, so did the need for more and better communication among personnel at the Lend-Lease transfer point. Fortunately, additional American foreign liaison interpreters were available for assignment to Ladd Field as winter arrived.

On November 25, George Kisevalter accompanied seven new interpreters to Fairbanks: Sergeants Baranoff, Chavchavadze, Chelnov, Dvoichenko-Markov, Gmirkin, Tumerin, and Wolston.[5] With their assignment, the I&I Russian section was at full interpreter strength for the first time. Kisevalter, the Russian section's commander, also now became the chief liaison officer at the base.

For David Chavchavadze, the trip to Fairbanks was filled with eager expectation. "In Alaska," he wrote, "I was meeting my first Soviets in person. It was enormously interesting to me." Despite his anti-Soviet background and rearing, Chavchavadze's attitude toward the Soviets was a positive one, and he professed "no feeling or resentment toward this generation of Soviets. If they liked the system they had, let them have it, was my attitude."[6]

As noted, new uniforms for the Red Air Force had been introduced several months earlier, with shoulder board insignia reminiscent of the those worn by the Russian imperial army. "It was a thrill when I saw my first Soviet officer. He was standing in front of a cigarette counter in the post exchange," Chavchavadze said. "[With his shoulder boards,] he looked so much like the countless photographs I had seen of my relatives in World War I.

"I was determined to work at my mission of facilitating good relations [with them]," he said. "I had no difficulty in talking with them. Some words and stresses were different, but there was no basic change in language." Although he tried to adapt to their way of speaking,

Three Soviet sergeants and Sgt. David Chavchavadze (*left*) in a snowball fight at Ladd Field, Alaska, 1943. Courtesy David Chavchavadze

Chavchavadze said he continued to receive compliments from them on the purity of his Russian.[7]

While en route to his Alaskan assignment, Chavchavadze had been worried that the Soviets would uncover his unusual background and aristocratic forebears, which he feared would make him a pariah. However, the opposite was true. "The Soviets [having somehow learned of my family history] turned out to be snobbish about the whole thing," he discovered. To Chavchavadze's surprise, some of the Soviets called him a "historical personality" and often referred to him as "Prince" or even "Comrade Prince"![8]

Captain Kisevalter appointed Chavchavadze to be the senior noncommissioned officer, in effect the first sergeant, of the I&I organization at Ladd Field. The appointment made sense because, unlike most of the other I&I interpreters with Russian backgrounds, Chavchavadze also had been thoroughly educated in English. He quickly became acquainted with military regulations and the handling of the I&I section's records and correspondence.

By virtue of his new position, Chavchavadze was able to meet the Soviet officers as well as enlisted men in the normal course of liaison operational activity at Ladd Field. During his nonduty hours, however, he was restricted to association with enlisted men; among the Soviets, most of these were mechanics.

"We ate together in the [central] mess, but otherwise there was almost no social life. The Soviet enlisted men never went to town [Fairbanks]," he said. "They must have been lonely and bored. Every night for almost two years there came from the enlisted barracks the sound of an accordion always mournfully playing the same Russian tune, *Siniy Platochek* (Little Blue Kerchief). This song always reminds me of Fairbanks and the iron curtain already present there."[9]

Part of the enlisted men's apparently self-imposed isolation presumably arose from compliance with the Soviet policy against fraternization in Fairbanks. Had they been inclined to go to Fairbanks for any reason, the tragic case of Sgt. Yevdokim Prozora served as a warning. When he became ill, Prozora was admitted to the Ladd Field station hospital. Chavchavadze, acting as interpreter, was present when Prozora was examined by an American medical officer. The desperate sergeant begged Chavchavadze to persuade the doctor to diagnose Prozora's ailment as being anything *except* venereal disease. The doctor, citing medical ethics, refused. Suffering from syphilis, Prozora was automatically assumed by his Soviet superiors to be guilty of fraternization with an Alaskan woman. Prozora protested hopelessly that he had been infected in Siberia before arriving in Alaska for duty. In the hospital, his only contact with a Russian-speaking person was with Chavchavadze, who visited him daily. "He acted like a condemned man, and he probably was," Chavchavadze said. Prozora later was returned to the Soviet Union, where he expected to be sent to almost certain death in a punishment battalion on the battlefield.[10]

Although the disciplined enlisted men lived under fear of punishment for carelessness or misbehavior, they endured what amounted to Alaskan exile without any sign of being tempted to desert. Kisevalter remembered that an officer (name withheld), in the course of a casual conversation at Ladd Field, asked Kisevalter how he could make a request to immigrate to America. Because Kisevalter did not believe that the question was an expression of intention to defect, he urged the officer not to pursue the subject further while the United States and the Soviet Union were military allies. Kisevalter advised that when the war was over, one could go to any American embassy in a neutral country and seek political asylum. The officer thanked Kisevalter for his counsel. To safeguard the officer, Kisevalter never reported the conversation.[11] Had any Soviet attempted to defect while in Alaska, the resulting diplomatic up-roar could have destroyed the usefulness of the ALSIB route.

Whether the efforts of the new I&I interpreters helped to ease ten-sions and suspicions among the Soviets was not readily determined, but nonetheless a change in the Soviets' behavior was soon detected. Proud and excited, the Soviets centered their attention and comments on the recent Red Army victories on the German front. They clamored for late war news from the I&I foreign liaison offices.

However, for unexplained reasons, Soviet security measures were re-tightened. The Soviets hedged their statements in conversations con-cerning ferrying operations to and base conditions in Siberia. Colonel Vasin, who himself in the past had often been indiscreet in his radio transmissions, issued new orders to tower operators and flight leaders not to disclose the number of aircraft in flight from Fairbanks to Nome. Operators also were ordered to cease providing uncoded weather reports between the tower at Nome and the one at Uel'kal.[12]

On December 6, the Soviet mechanics at Nome sponsored a dinner to honor their ATC counterparts. In all, twenty-two American mechan-ics and engineers were invited to join in the festive gathering to express Soviet appreciation for American help in servicing and expediting Lend-Lease aircraft scheduled to enter Siberia. The Soviet invitation undoubt-edly was a genuine gesture of gratitude. At both Nome and Fairbanks, the Soviet Military Mission was beginning to feel the pinch of a short-age of mechanics, but especially at Nome.[13]

Lt. Gen. L. G. Rudenko, the new chairman of the Soviet Purchasing Com-mission in Washington, arrived at Nome from Moscow via the ALSIB route on December 13. In his conversation with General Jones, Rudenko said he was impressed with the ferry operation that he observed during his flight across Siberia. The ALSIB route, he said, ensured the fastest means of moving aircraft to the battlefield. He added that the ALSIB route's con-tinued operation must not be jeopardized.

Rudenko arrived at Nome an ill man. Although he was able to fly to Fairbanks on December 14, he was confined to bed rest at Ladd Field for three days. By December 17 his health had improved sufficiently for him to resume his trip to Washington.[14] Among other projects in Washing-ton, he soon began to negotiate the volume and priorities of Lend-Lease aircraft to be delivered during the forthcoming Fourth Protocol period.

On September 11, a massive American bombing strike had been sent against Japan's strongholds in the northern Kurile Islands. The Japanese

Left to right: Colonel Machin, Lieutenant General Rudenko (new chief of the Soviet Purchasing Commission in Washington) and Brigadier General Jones meet in Nome, December 13, 1943. Courtesy Col. Louis Klam

defenders downed three of the raiding bombers and damaged seven others, which crash-landed in Soviet neutral territory on the Kamchatka Peninsula.[15] Maj. C. G. Wagner was the pilot of one of the crashed bombers. The fifty-one surviving airmen from the crash-landings on Kamchatka, including Wagner and his crew, were interned by the Soviets. In October, the airmen were moved across Siberia to an internment holding camp in south-central Asia near Tashkent. En route to the camp, the internees were first flown to Khabarovsk. Their aerial odyssey then followed the Trans-Siberian Railroad corridor westward to Krasnoyarsk, where they saw row on row of Lend-Lease fighters and bombers at the ALSIB route's termination base.[16]

In early December, Wakov D. Gorbenko was a Soviet bomber pilot assigned to ferrying duty on the ALSIB route. By an unexplained set of circumstances, Gorbenko arrived at Nome from Yakutsk bearing a piece of rough paper on which was a handwritten note signed by Major Wagner. He wrote that he and his crew had been interned but well treated and were in good health. Wagner asked that his note be passed to his wife, Mrs. Christine Wagner, of 629 West 138th Street, New York City.[17]

Krasnoyarsk was the only point in Siberia where it was possible for him to contact ALSIB route pilots. During the internees' overnight stop at Krasnoyarsk, they were guests of Red Air Force flyers at a banquet held at the air base. Gorbenko himself was not present at the banquet; he was on furlough at Yakutsk, 1,400 miles away. In some manner, however, Wagner passed the note to a Soviet airman, perhaps an ALSIB route pilot, who carried it to Yakutsk. Gorbenko said he was given the note by an unidentified person at Yakutsk.[18]

Wagner's note was the only clandestine U.S. message known to have been smuggled from Siberia to Alaska during World War II. The ALSIB flyers who carried it from Krasnoyarsk played a dangerous game, as did Gorbenko, to avoid NKVD detection.

As Christmas approached, the Soviet Military Mission, having obtained permission to bring wives and children of selected senior officers to Alaska, still was unable to locate any additional housing for the families. The mission tried to lease three houses and, in an unprecedented move, even offered to make outright purchases of the houses—valued at thirty thousand dollars each (1943 dollars)—with no success. Availability of funds for Soviet purchases of this magnitude did not appear to be a problem.[19]

Neither was there a shortage of monies for the personal use of the Soviets assigned to duty in the Alaskan "colony." They eagerly bought native craft items that they boxed in holiday gift wrappings. Eskimo mukluks [boots] especially were in demand. Christmas cards, considered souvenirs, were also purchased for sending to friends and families in the Soviet Union.[20]

During the final weeks of 1943, the three Air Force service squadrons acquired by ATC were in place at Edmonton, Whitehorse, and Nome. With their presence, the ATC's Alaskan Wing established an improved maintenance and supply organization along the Northwest route corridor and at Nome.[21] Hangars at stations along the route were either completed or in final construction stages.[22]

While the ATC was now able to operate its ferry route with adequate service facilities, the Soviets began to fret about their own service problems, especially the shortage of mechanics and engineers. Some improvements were noted at their Siberian bases. Timbers were used to construct sleeping quarters to replace the sod-covered huts at Uel'kal and elsewhere. Hangar construction, however, did not have any special priority. Instead, mechanics still serviced aircraft in the open air, even during the worst of winter conditions. Mechanics at Uel'kal, Markovo, and Seymchan wore fur coveralls and fur face masks while working on bombers and fighters that were covered with heavy cotton tarpaulin-type blankets for warmth.[23]

When ferry operations entered the bitter winter season in January, 1944, the extreme temperatures were expected to slow the volume of aircraft deliveries. However, ATC started the new year with a stable flow of airplanes only slightly below Third Protocol commitments. Colonel Mazuruk reported from Siberia that the only major problem that his ALSIB ferrying division was encountering was the tendency of retractable landing gear to malfunction due to the extreme cold. He called for a technical conference to be held at Ladd Field to address the problem. Attending were mechanics and engineers from the Uel'kal to Yakutsk portion of the ALSIB route.[24]

As 1944 arrived, the Soviet colony in Alaska reached its peak strength with 160 civilians, military personnel, and dependents there (appendix B). Although changes occurred in the names on the personnel rosters, the overall numbers of permanent personnel remained near the same throughout the coming year despite vacancies in certain technical positions.

In February, the Red Air Force announced for "troops on foreign duty" a personnel rotation policy that could apply to the members of the Soviet Military Mission in Alaska. The basic criteria for rotation eligibility included two years of service outside the Soviet Union. Since the first Soviets had arrived in Alaska in September, 1942, adherence to the two-year rule would delay the beginning of rotation until September, seven months hence. Nevertheless, two officers (Peter I. Ozhogov and Vladimir G. Doubovitsky, both junior technical lieutenants) were announced as the first to go. Therefore, the application of the two years of service appeared to be a guideline open to various interpretations.[25]

The early loss of two officers would not in itself seem to be crucial. If the officers were aviators, the loss could be handled readily by replacements from the pool of airmen due for rest from combat. But these two officers were engineers; obtaining qualified replacements in the near future was doubtful. Colonel Kiselev had been protesting the shortage of mechanics and engineers for some time, and he foresaw that the continuing drain of technical personnel could soon have an adverse effect on the ALSIB route operation.[26]

Soviet officers, especially those who had arrived in Alaska in 1942, began to make plans to return "home." With the favorable war news of the Red Army's sweeping successes, even the recent Soviet arrivals expressed their belief that their stay in Alaska would be a short one. The war, they said, could not last longer than a few more months.[27]

Despite the excellent delivery record in January, frigid weather in Canada slowed ATC deliveries during February and March to 80 percent of the monthly commitments. The Soviets' ALSIB route deliveries slowed even more and in some instances came to a virtual standstill. While much of the disruption was attributable to adverse weather in Siberia, Colonel Kiselev apparently sensed that human problems within the Soviet organization at Ladd Field were also to blame.

Kiselev had ample reason to be concerned about the personnel shortages in his technical services ranks. He was concerned, too, about the developing bottleneck in the Soviet inspection and transfer procedures. Seeking an independent view, Kiselev used his Soviet technical channel to General Rudenko's office in Washington. He asked Rudenko "to send a good man to Ladd Field to look at the situation objectively." In Kiselev's opinion, "the situation could hardly be worse."[28]

As the Siberian weather conditions improved, so did the movement of aircraft. In the meantime, Soviet inspectors from Washington were reported to have placed blame for some of the ALSIB route's operational problems on five cumulative factors:[29]

1. A shortage of engineering personnel, about which Kiselev had already complained.
2. Lack of sufficient clerical help to prepare the increasing volume of inspection and transfer records.
3. Excessive use of ferrying crews to fly high-ranking Soviet officials all the way to Moscow. Use of pilots and crews for this purpose removed them from essential ferrying assignments for as long as two months at a time.
4. A breakdown in administrative and technical coordination within the Soviet organization at Ladd Field. This appeared to be the first hint that coordination problems had developed between the Soviet Purchasing Commission office and the Soviet Military Mission.
5. Jealousies between the high-ranking Soviet officials at Ladd Field. Specific identities were not mentioned, but among the senior officials were A. A. Anisimov, Colonel Machin, Colonel Kiselev, and Colonel Vasin, the latter having recently been promoted from lieutenant colonel.

By late May, presumably as the result of remedial action, Kiselev informed his superiors in Washington that as a whole the situation at Ladd Field had reached a satisfactory state, with the exception of the availability and use of transports. He estimated that eighty transports would be required to haul the regularly scheduled cargo during the months of June, July, and August, 1944. Kiselev in addition complained about the excessive number of passengers that were being booked for flights through Alaska.[30]

Even when the ALSIB route first became operational and the facilities and accommodations at the Siberian bases were primitive, dangerous, and uncomfortable, the route had an irresistible attraction for important officials, mostly Soviet. The attraction was the time element. This route provided the quickest avenue for travel between Moscow and Washington in both directions.

During the eighteen months since the international air route had been established, the condition of the Siberian bases had steadily improved and the passenger traffic steadily increased. Ambassadors, generals, diplomats, and political personalities all passed through Alaska in what seemed an endless stream. The more important the passenger, the more attention he needed, especially for unscheduled air travel, putting the ferrying schedules at risk.

The highest-ranking official to travel the ALSIB route was not a Soviet but Henry A. Wallace, vice president of the United States. Wallace departed Washington on May 20, 1944, to begin a special mission to China. The White House announced that the vice president would also visit the Siberian city of Krasnoyarsk and the Soviet south Asian city of Tashkent.[31]

Wallace and his staff traveled in a special military transport with a crew of seven. From Washington they flew to Edmonton for an overnight rest stop. Here General Gaffney, identified as the commander of the ATC's Alaskan Wing, greeted the vice president.

Wallace resumed his trip the next day over the Northwest route to Ladd Field, where he held a press conference and praised the manner in which Americans and Soviets together were making the Lend-Lease ferry route function effectively. He lauded the ATC's Alaskan Wing for meeting "its present responsibilities" in delivering airplanes to the Soviets at Fairbanks.[32] Unlike the censors' usual practice of delaying the release of sensitive news stories for weeks or even months, the Wallace stories from Washington, Edmonton, and Fairbanks were released promptly.

From Fairbanks, the vice president's plane followed the ALSIB route across Siberia all the way to Krasnoyarsk. At his Siberian visits, Wallace discussed agricultural production problems with Soviet specialists and then flew eastward from Tashkent[33] to Chungking, China, for meetings with Chiang Kai-shek. On his return trip, Wallace rejoined the ALSIB route and followed it to Fairbanks, arriving on July 4.[34]

Vice President Henry A. Wallace with Col. N. S. Vasin (USSR) and Col. Russell Keillor, Ladd Field commander, at dinner during Wallace's stopover at Fairbanks during his 1944 mission to the Soviet Union and China via the ALSIB route. Courtesy National Archives

By the time Wallace departed Alaska the next day and again flew over the Northwest route, his published statements had exposed, either by design or by accident, a wider view of the U.S. ferrying activities not previously revealed to the American public. Following the vice president's return to Washington, the War Department lifted the official restrictions on the details of Northwest route operations. The ATC was therefore free to disclose and discuss its own role in the Lend-Lease ferrying activities over the Northwest route.[35]

Two versions of the Soviet red star insignia painted on each Siberia-bound airplane were now seen: one was the usual red star superimposed on a white disk; the other was a red star with a narrow white border on it.[36] Photographs of Lend-Lease planes openly bearing the red stars began to appear in U.S. periodicals. Information regarding the Soviets' portion of the ferrying route across Siberia, however, remained closely held by the Soviet Military Mission.

Apparently the Red Air Force's rotation policy was responsible for plucking the Soviet Military Mission's commanding officer, Colonel

Machin, from his Alaskan assignment. He had arrived with the original cadre of Soviet personnel in September, 1942, to establish the critically important Soviet outpost at Fairbanks, and on his shoulders rested the responsibility for ensuring that the Soviet-American marriage of convenience in Alaska was successful. Now, nineteen months later, he was returning to Moscow and reassignment that would bring high honors and promotion.

On April 19, American officers at Ladd Field sponsored a farewell party for Machin. In the midst of the festivities, a gift shotgun was presented to the guest of honor, who was known for his hunting zeal. He also was given a book containing autographs of the American officers with whom he had been associated. Machin responded on May 1 with a rowdy party at which the supply of vodka and Soviet sentimentality seemed inexhaustible. Then on May 9, after a brief ceremony, Machin, his wife, and their sons stepped aboard a Soviet transport at Ladd field and were gone.[37]

On July 14, President Roosevelt approved the award of the Legion of Merit medal honoring Colonel Machin for his leadership, cooperation, and service during his stressful period of duty in Alaska.[38] The Soviets referred to the medal under a related title of "Legion of Valor."

Colonel Kiselev, who had acted for Machin during the latter's absence in August and September, 1943, again assumed responsibility for the Soviet Military Mission until a new commander arrived later in 1944. In his dual assignment as chief of engineering and inspection services as well as executive officer, Kiselev was intimately acquainted with the mission's operations. His U.S. associates were especially pleased to have the mission in Kiselev's hands, even if temporarily, because of the officer's usually calm and reasonable approach to Soviet-American relations.

Lt. Elena Makarova, one of the mission's senior technical interpreters, likewise departed for Moscow a month later, on June 2.[39] She too had been in Alaska since the inception of the mission. Although Makarova had promised to marry the flamboyant bomber squadron commander Peter Gamov in 1943, they had not married when she departed, leaving Gamov in Alaska until the end of the war.[40] Their romance persisted, however. Her replacement in her Alaskan post was Lt. Naum I. Slobodskoy, a technical officer who was fluent in English and who had once served as an aide to Colonel Machin.

Makarova's companion technical interpreter, Lt. Natasha Fenelonova, also remained in Alaska until the Soviet Military Mission was dissolved at the end of the war (chap. 10).

The Red Air Force's personnel rotation policy was not unique. For American military assignment purposes, the War Department considered Alaska to be an overseas area. Therefore, after two years of service in Alaska, an American serviceman became eligible for reassignment. Capt. George Kisevalter, the chief liaison officer at Ladd Field and commander of the I&I Russian section, fell into this category.

As anticipated, Kisevalter was ordered to report for duty with the War Department General Staff (G-2) in Washington on June 1, 1944. Both Igor Gubert at Nome and Michael Gavrisheff at Fairbanks were performing their foreign liaison duties in an outstanding manner. Gavrisheff had been and Gubert soon would be promoted to the grade of captain. With the departure of Kisevalter, a logical adjustment in the I&I Russian section's command structure was made to avoid a major relocation of key officers. Gubert remained as the foreign liaison officer-in-charge at Nome, and Gavrisheff, having understudied Kisevalter at Ladd Field, became the chief liaison officer at Ladd Field and the I&I Russian section's commander.

In anticipation of Kisevalter's reassignment, the Alaskan Department requisitioned a replacement to fill the liaison officer's position vacated by Gavrisheff. The replacement, Lt. Kyrill de Shishmareff, arrived on schedule shortly before Kisevalter's departure. General consternation reigned, however, when de Shishmareff, despite his illustrious Russian forebears, revealed that he did not speak Russian. Urgent cables were sent to Washington in a frantic effort to obtain a qualified language officer from the replacement pipeline. In the meantime, Gavrisheff found that he could depend on Sergeant Chavchavadze to help with the liaison problems that were mounting at Ladd Field because of the officer shortage.[41]

The last days of ferrying operations to fulfill the Third Protocol commitments, still somewhat behind schedule, were approaching. Both the Soviet Military Mission and the ATC were alerted to the Soviets' adoption of a new Lend-Lease fighter, and training and operational adjustments were planned to ease the integration of the newcomer into the ferrying program.

The newcomer was the P-63 Kingcobra. Similar in appearance to the P-39 Airacobra, it was in fact an updated and more potent replacement for that popular Lend-Lease fighter. In February, 1944, three of the P-63s had been shipped to the Soviet Union for testing. Satisfied with the trial results, the Soviets issued final instructions to phase out the faithful P-39 in favor of the P-63. The changeover was announced to begin soon.[42]

Later in June, 1944, even as the first of the new fighters was arriving at Great Falls to enter the Northwest route, Colonel Kiselev was faced with an assortment of problems, one of which was a special Lend-Lease cargo reported to be at Ladd Field. The Soviet Military Mission was requested to locate the missing cargo and forward it over the ALSIB route as quickly as possible. The special cargo contained spare parts for the three P-63 fighters already in Soviet hands. Since the P-63 parts were not interchangeable with those of the P-39, the need for the spare parts was urgent.[43] Unfortunately, other difficulties with the P-63 would soon reach major proportions.

Beginning on June 14, the first P-63 fighter was delivered to Ladd Field, and thirty-five more followed during the remainder of the month. The new arrivals also brought new problems involving fresh transition training for the Soviet ferry pilots and orientation technical instruction for the mechanics. Although experienced P-39 pilots needed only thirty minutes of flying time for their P-63 transition training, the mechanics' orientation was much more time-consuming.[44]

June 30, 1944, was the final day for deliveries of Lend-Lease aircraft to fulfill the Third Protocol commitments, and the year-long count of aircraft arriving at the Fairbanks transfer point was 3,279. This Third Protocol volume was approximately three times greater than the inaugural Second Protocol volume between September, 1942, and June, 1943.[45]

By the end of June in 1944, twenty-six of the new P-63 Kingcobras had been flown as far as Nome but, as of that time, none of the aircraft had yet been formally transferred to the Soviets. Therefore, none of the P-63s had entered Siberia.

9.
The End
in Sight

In 1941 when the rampaging German armies slashed through the Red Army's defenses, another calamity lurked in the Soviet Far East: an invasion by Japan's powerful Kwantung Army poised in Manchuria. In those desperate times of 1941 and 1942, the Soviet-Japanese neutrality pact of April, 1941, offered solace to the Soviet Union but no guarantee against unexpected Japanese aggression.

By 1943, however, the tide of battle was turning against Germany. The Red Army stood fast at Stalingrad and the relentless counterattack began to move westward. At the same time, Japan was feeling the beginning of the Allied offensive in her South Pacific outposts and in the outer Aleutian Islands. Before the year was out, the Japanese forces were mired in an endless defensive island war of attrition. Month by month, the Kwantung Army in Manchuria gradually presented a declining invasion threat to the Soviet Union.

By mid-October of 1943, the future role of the Soviet Union in the Pacific surfaced for the first time. The U.S., British, and Soviet foreign ministers—Cordell Hull, Anthony Eden, and V. M. Molotov—met in Moscow. Among the conference achievements was a pledge to establish a new organization for world peace after the war. Stalin met with the ministers and made an unsolicited pledge that the Soviet Union would join the Allies against Japan after the defeat of Germany.[1] Averill Harriman, the new U.S. ambassador to the Soviet Union, reported to Roosevelt that "they [the Soviets] no longer appear to fear Japan."[2]

The foreign ministers laid the groundwork for the summit meeting of Roosevelt, Churchill, and Stalin in Tehran, Iran, in November.[3] The Big Three discussions did not elaborate on the Soviet plans in the Pacific war but instead concentrated on coordination of blows against the German armies when the future Allied landings were made in western Europe. Stalin, in an expansive statement at the closing dinner on November 30, said that without the miracle of American production, the war would have been lost.[4]

The summer of 1944 saw momentous events in the conduct of World War II. The Allied landings in Normandy and southern France were successfully made while the Red Army continued to roll the retreating German forces westward. In the Pacific, the island-hopping Allied forces were on the offensive, and the early mass bombing raids on the Japanese homeland were launched.

Soviet-American operations in Alaska inevitably felt the ripples of the war's larger events, and the changes that had begun in the early part of 1944 now quickened. In effect, many of the operational changes were overdue because both the U.S. and Soviet ferrying organizations at last were reaching maturity. General Rudenko in Washington reflected Soviet confidence in the successful operation of the ALSIB route: he announced that all Lend-Lease aircraft listed in the new Fourth Protocol would be delivered over the ALSIB route exclusively.[5]

The Air Transport Command, recognizing the expanded responsibilities of its Alaskan Wing, elevated the ferrying organization from wing to division status. On July 1, the ATC's Alaskan Division assumed the former wing's functions without any change in boundaries or command.[6]

Both Americans and Soviets geared themselves to handle the flow of aircraft scheduled for transfer during the ensuing months of 1944 and 1945. The Fourth Protocol called for delivery of 2,940 aircraft in addition to those still obligated under previous protocols. Beginning in July, ATC began the process of providing the Soviets at Ladd Field with a record-breaking total of 3,538 fighter, bomber, transport, and trainer aircraft during the final period of Soviet-American collaboration in Alaska.

As requested by General Rudenko, the new P-63 Kingcobra fighters would comprise 60 percent of the Fourth Protocol deliveries. Soviet aircraft production, together with the changing requirements for aircraft in the Red Air Force, influenced the Soviets' interest in acquiring the new American fighter. The Red Air Force no longer felt the need for the A-20 light bomber and therefore, after the delivery of forty-one in July, suspended any further orders. The actual phasing out of the P-39 Airacobra fighters began in August. The P-39 deliveries were completed in September when the Soviet Military Mission accepted the last twelve of them.[7]

The changeover to the P-63 fighter was not a simple one. As in the case of new types of aircraft, problems developed that were not discovered in the testing and early mass production phases. Although the first group of new P-63s had arrived in June and been divided between Nome and Fairbanks, the Soviet inspectors considered them to be unacceptable. The fighters therefore were grounded until mechanical and performance problems could be solved to the Soviets' satisfaction.

Among the Soviets' complaints were discoveries of cracking fuel booster pumps, breaking selector valves, breaking rudder control housings, and unreliable rudder controls. Temporary expedients were used to correct the problems. In July, the P-63s were considered airworthy, but the Soviet Military Mission demanded assurances that the factory would provide improved replacement parts.[8]

While the corrections were being made on the original group of fighters, ATC delivered 304 mixed types of Lend-Lease craft, including an additional seventy-eight P-63s. In August, ATC established a Lend-Lease record for the number of airplanes delivered to Fairbanks in a single month—a total of 403, of which 270 were more P-63s. The August record would never be broken. September was another high delivery month with 350 additional arrivals, the P-63 portion amounting to 218.[9]

On September 10, as the first September arrivals were logged into Ladd Field, a P-63 became the 5,000th Lend-Lease airplane to be delivered to the Soviets since the establishment of the ALSIB route.[10]

Beginning in early October, however, the delivery of aircraft abruptly came to a near standstill for the first time since December of 1942. A scheduled flow of twenty-two transports (C-47) and forty bombers (B-25) reached Fairbanks. But instead of the expected arrival of about 275 fighters (P-63), only thirty-one landed to join hundreds of the fighters again grounded at Fairbanks and Nome. The reason: the Soviet Military Mission refused to accept any of the fighters until a major essential modification was made.

According to the Soviets, after they had accepted the new fighter when its earlier problems had been corrected in July, their subsequent experience revealed a disastrous fuselage structural weakness. With the major portion of the ALSIB route paralyzed by the grounding action, the Army Air Force and the Bell Aircraft Corporation, manufacturer of the P-63, called an emergency conference in which an agreement was reached to undertake the massive task of strengthening the fuselages of the stalled aircraft immediately. As a result, modification materials and some 125 civilian mechanics, factory representatives, and inspectors were hastily assembled and flown to Alaska. Around-the-clock work began at Fairbanks and Nome on October 19. The fuselage modifications were completed twelve days later, on November 1.

Soviet officials also asked for a ventral fin to be installed on the underside of each fuselage. When advised that the fin could not be made available for another six weeks, the Soviets waived the requirement. On November 10, the jam of grounded P-63s eased as the fighters again were scheduled to traverse Siberia.[11]

In the midst of the ALSIB route's paralysis caused by the grounded P-63s, the departure of General Jones from Nome on October 4 was not a complete surprise. Jones had become commander of the military forces at Nome in 1942 when the Seward Peninsula was considered in imminent danger of being invaded. Two years later, the presence of an army general officer was no longer justified, and Jones released his diminished garrison command to Lt. Col. William T. Kirn.

With the general's departure, Captain Gubert and his I&I liaison team of interpreters entered a new period of adjustment with the ATC command that, fortunately, did not directly interrupt their established liaison with the Soviets. However, the general's departure visibly dismayed the Soviets, to whom Jones had become a sort of father figure, a friend to come to their rescue whenever they had an unsolved problem at Nome.[12]

The Soviet government, undoubtedly influenced by reports from Colonel Vasin and his fellow senior officers in Alaska, honored General Jones with the award of the Order of Suvorov, the highest Soviet medal given to foreigners. The Alaskan Department also awarded General Jones the Legion of Merit medal.[13]

As the month of May, 1944, came to a close, the I&I Russian section's interpreters at Ladd Field faced mounting demands for their services. The liaison section still lacked a qualified second officer to replace Lieutenant de Shishmareff, and the shortage soon created problems.

For example, when two assigned liaison officers were on duty at Ladd Field, one of them was available to escort Soviet diplomatic missions and delegations en route from Moscow through Alaska to Canada or

At Nome in 1944, dozens of P-63 fighters await official Soviet clearance before leaving for their hazardous flight across Siberia. Courtesy Army Air Force

the United States. In addition to Russian-speaking escorts, American pilots also were assigned to assist the Soviet pilots in entering and using the Canadian and American airways.

"There were times when I flew with the Soviets across Canada when flying was inadvisable," Captain Gavrisheff recalled. "On two such occasions we had to fly under a low cloud cover through narrow valleys so that we could maintain visual contact with the rivers below." Both times, he said, the Soviets were advised against flying but insisted "that the Soviet pilots knew best." Crashes were miraculously averted "despite the bullheadedness and lack of prudence on the part of the Soviet crews."[14]

Although the reassigned George Kisevalter was ready to depart, Gavrisheff was again absent from Ladd Field, having been detailed to escort a Soviet delegation to Montreal. The Soviet and American crews, together with Gavrisheff, were instructed to take the Soviet transport via New York City to Washington, there to await further orders. By telephone from Montreal, Gavrisheff arranged for his Washington girlfriend to meet him in New York City so that she could ride in a Soviet airplane with him to Washington. "She thought it was a lark," Gavrisheff said, "and the Soviet crew thought it an honor."[15]

When Gavrisheff returned to Ladd Field, Kisevalter was gone and the requested Russian-speaking replacement for Lieutenant de Shishmareff was still not available. As July neared, Gavrisheff vainly waited for a proper replacement. The midsummer bustle of ferrying activity and the increased official passenger traffic placed added pressure on Gavrisheff to consider an alternate solution.

Since Alaska was still designated as an official combat zone, the commanding general of the Alaskan Department had the authority to commission qualified enlisted men as officers when extraordinary circumstances existed. On July 3, Lt. Gen. Simon B. Buckner, Jr., commanding general, received an urgent application for the field-commissioning of Sgt. David Chavchavadze.

In the letter that Captain Gavrisheff, as commander of the I&I Russian section, wrote to justify the application, he noted Chavchavadze's aristocratic Russian and Georgian heritage, his fluency in Russian, his exemplary record of service at Ladd Field, his cultural education in the United States, and his military intelligence training. He also emphasized Chavchavadze's demonstrated ease in meeting and working with foreigners and Americans alike. Gavrisheff cautioned, "Do not be misled by Chavchavadze's [youthful] age. He is quite mature."[16]

The application was approved.

"It was unbelievable," Chavchavadze wrote. "On a Sunday morning [July 23], some sergeant woke me up and summoned me to Ladd Field's base headquarters. . . . I found myself [at the age of twenty] being sworn in as a second lieutenant in the Army of the United States. . . . On Sundays, the post exchange was closed, so I could not buy insignia. Kyrill [de Shishmareff] gave me insignia, and clothes too, to get me by as an officer. I walked into my barracks to collect my worldly goods. I was immediately surrounded by my friends who demanded to know, in Russian, if I was out of my mind [to be] impersonating an officer!"[17] A few days later, Lieutenant de Shishmareff departed for a nonlinguistic assignment in the continental United States.

Within three weeks of his field-commissioning, Lieutenant Chavchavadze was put to his first major test. In mid-August, Ambassador Andrei Gromyko arrived at Ladd Field en route to Washington for the Dumbarton Oaks Conference, one of the Soviet-British-American planning sessions leading eventually to the charter for the United Nations Organization. Gromyko's party contained a staff of nineteen Soviet bureaucrats and a flight crew of three—Soviet pilot, engineer, and radio operator. At Ladd Field, an American pilot, radio operator, and liaison interpreter (Chavchavadze) joined the Soviet crew.

With good flying weather all the way, the Soviet diplomatic plane made three routine landings along the Northwest route and then continued to Minneapolis. The tired Soviet crew wanted an overnight rest stop and asked Chavchavadze to approach Gromyko and get his approval. At first, the ambassador brushed aside the request, saying he did not want to risk being late for his Washington arrival appointment with Edward Stettinius, undersecretary of state. With Chavchavadze's persuasion, however, he reluctantly agreed. He specified one firm condition: that the flight to Washington must resume promptly at 5:00 A.M.

After lodging the ambassador's party at a convenient hotel, the Americans were free to explore the city's night life. The radio operator announced that this was his birthday, and he was eager to celebrate it.

Adhering to Gromyko's instructions, Chavchavadze was present at the ambassador's hotel at 4:00 A.M. to escort the Soviet party aboard a bus and go to the airfield in time to depart as scheduled. The American pilot arrived and took his seat in the cockpit with his Soviet counterpart, but the American radio operator was missing. A frantic telephone call to his hotel awakened the sleepy radioman, who had celebrated his birthday all too well. As the groggy radioman later scrambled into the plane, an exasperated Gromyko demanded that Chavchavadze explain why his departure orders had not been obeyed.

It was now 6:00 A.M. Chavchavadze had spent the waiting time since 5:00 A.M. considering various alibis to cope with Gromyko's anticipated wrath. He finally decided simply to tell the truth about the radioman's birthday celebration. "To my surprise," Chavchavadze said, "the stern face relaxed into a smile, and Gromyko actually chuckled." Chavchavadze wondered, however, whether Gromyko really understood and sympathized, or whether the chuckle was caused by the thought of what he would have done to a Soviet radio operator under similar circumstances.

While the Dumbarton Oaks Conference was in session, Chavchavadze planned a visit from Washington to New York, where he hoped to surprise his mother at her home. She was not surprised. Her attention had already been called to a news story mentioning the fact that Gromyko's liaison officer on this trip was a relative of Emperor Nicholas II![18] Chavchavadze returned to Ladd Field in September to resume the less heady duties expected of a newly commissioned junior liaison officer.

Meanwhile, the Dumbarton Oaks Conference in Washington continued until October 9. Each representative presented proposals for the international peace organization that included a Security Council and an United Nations Assembly. The question of membership in the assembly, however, was not resolved because Gromyko insisted that each of the sixteen republics of the Soviet Union should be allowed individual membership with voting rights.[19]

Following Chavchavadze's return, a group of senior Allied military attachés accredited to their Canadian embassies at Ottawa visited Ladd Field. Chavchavadze learned quickly that even as an officer, his liaison duties as an interpreter had unexpected hazards.

"I had a run-in with Colonel Vasin [the commander of the 1st Ferrying Aviation Regiment based at Ladd Field]," he said. "There was a big banquet for the attachés. As the junior liaison officer, I had to interpret. The Soviets were hosts and I was seated next to Colonel Vasin." The ritual vodka toasting to Allied unity was offered again and again. Trying to remain sober enough to perform his duties, Chavchavadze in desperation finally resorted to tossing his vodka drinks past his ear and over his shoulder to the wall behind him. Nobody seemed to notice, nobody except Colonel Vasin.

Taking Chavchavadze's action as a personal insult, Vasin told him furiously, "Your ancestors were honorable Russian officers. If you were under my command, I would have you shot for that!"

He was not kidding, Chavchavadze said. "Colonel Vasin never addressed a pleasant word to me after that evening."[20]

Gavrisheff likewise encountered unexpected difficulties, although his were personal. In November, an international conference on postwar civil aviation agreements was scheduled to be convened in Chicago. The Soviet delegation of four generals and their NKVD escort arrived from Moscow at Ladd Field. Chief of the delegation was Lt. Gen. A. A. Avseyevich, the same general who had come to Nome and Fairbanks in 1943 to investigate Soviet-American relations on Stalin's behalf. While the delegation was en route from Moscow, the Soviet government decided not to participate in the conference unless the delegations of "fascist nations" were excluded.

Captain Gavrisheff was selected as the Soviet delegation's escort and interpreter for the flight from Alaska to Chicago. However, while the Soviet government's demand was being considered by the conference's sponsors, the Soviet delegation was diverted to Winnipeg, Canada, where the generals and Gavrisheff waited for developments.

No compromise was reached. The Soviet delegation was directed back to Alaska, and from there to Moscow.

The diplomatic stalemate and confusion wrecked Gavrisheff's personal plans. Had the delegation convened in Chicago as expected, Gavrisheff and his fiancée in Washington planned to be married while he was idle during the course of the conference. When Gavrisheff was ordered to accompany the Soviet delegation back to Alaska, his bride-to-be was forced to cancel the formal wedding scheduled at St. Alban's church in Washington. By telephone from Winnipeg, Gavrisheff told her, "I swear to you that I am due back to Washington in the spring [1945] and that would be the time to be married."

But it was not to be. She married an air force officer a year later.[21]

With the successful landing of the Allied forces in France in June of 1944 and the defeat of Germany in sight, the time and place of the next Big Three meeting was now open to negotiation. Roosevelt had been considering a summer meeting in Fairbanks. However, because of his preoccupation with the approaching November general election in which he was seeking a fourth term, he wanted to wait until after the election. By that time, it would be too late and too cold for traveling and meeting in Alaska. Instead, Roosevelt proposed a late November meeting somewhere in the warm Mediterranean area.

Stalin rejected the proposed site. His doctors, he said, would not allow him to travel so far.

Churchill decided not to wait until Roosevelt and Stalin solved their personal problems. If necessary, he would go alone to Moscow. One of his objectives was to establish, once and for all, whether the Soviets seriously intended to enter the war against Japan.[22]

Stalin agreed to meet with Churchill in mid-October. Roosevelt, who considered the Moscow meeting to be preliminary to a full-scale Big Three summit, arranged for Ambassador Harriman and General Deane, chief of the U.S. Military Mission to Moscow, to be present for the Churchill-Stalin discussions. In response to Deane's questions, Stalin announced that the Soviet armed forces would enter the war with Japan three months after the end of the German war. The three-month period, he said, was needed to move additional Red Army divisions to the Far East and to develop a million-ton stockpile of supplies (including Lend-Lease items) in Siberia. He also agreed to the eventual establishment of American air bases in the Maritime Provinces, to the use of Petropavlovsk as an American naval base, and to begin joint operational planning.[23]

When Roosevelt, Churchill, and Stalin met at Yalta in the Crimea in early February, 1945, Stalin reiterated his earlier pledge to enter the war against Japan three months after the collapse of Germany. American military planners anticipated that Soviet involvement in the war would prevent Japan from moving its Kwantung Army from Manchuria to Japan's home island defenses.[24]

Stalin planned, in coordination with the Chinese, to drive the Japanese from Manchuria and North China, and for this he expected the restoration of certain rights and territories that Japan had taken from Russia in 1905. In addition, Stalin sought repossession of the Kurile Islands, which Russia had ceded to Japan in 1875. The U.S. delegation at Yalta, offering no objection to Stalin's plans and expectations, seemed well satisfied with the bargain.[25]

The Big Three also decided to call a conference at San Francisco in April to produce the United Nations Organization charter. Foreign Minister Molotov announced that the Soviet Union was ready to accept the American formula for voting in the Security Council, a formula that the Soviets had earlier resisted. In return, Roosevelt and Churchill agreed to allow Stalin three votes in the General Assembly—by the USSR, Ukraine, and Byelorussia (also referred to as White Russia and currently as Belarus)—scaled down from the earlier Soviet demand at Dumbarton Oaks that each of the sixteen republics be given a vote.[26]

Beginning in late March, 1944, Kodiak's naval air station, the scene of the first official aerial Alaska-Siberian reconnection in 1941, again played host to Soviet military airmen, this time those of the navy. Fifty pilots and crewmen arrived at Fairbanks on March 30 after an eight-day flight from Moscow. U.S. Navy air transports shuttled the Soviet aviators first to Kodiak, thence all the way to Elizabeth City, North Carolina. From Elizabeth City, the Soviet crews prepared to ferry forty-eight PBY Catalina flying boats to the Soviet Union. Most of them were flown over the North route via Iceland. The others were flown over the South route via Brazil, North Africa, and Iran. The Lend-Lease deliveries were completed in June.[27]

In addition to the PBY flying boats, the Soviet Navy asked for and was allocated ninety PBN-type patrol seaplanes. Sixty of them were scheduled for delivery via Iceland at the rate of five per month. The other thirty, however, were to be flown from Alaska over a special Soviet Navy ferry route. Having no relationship to the ALSIB route, this separate ferrying operation was a temporary one established only to deliver the seaplanes via Anadyr to Magadan, Siberia.

On August 10, 1944, a select group of fifty Soviet Navy aviators arrived at Kodiak to receive the first of the Lend-Lease seaplanes being delivered by U.S. Navy pilots. Lt. Col. V. Tertsiev, in charge of the Soviet project, consulted with American officials at Kodiak and then assembled his staff and flew to Fairbanks. There they also consulted with Soviet and ATC officials about codes, charts, and radio frequencies as well as the suitability of Anadyr's refueling facilities on the Siberian coast. Returning to Kodiak, Tertsiev then completed his plans for the ferry operation.

On August 25, the first group of seaplanes manned by their Soviet crews departed Kodiak for the pioneering flight. After a ten-hour passage over the Alaska Peninsula and the Bering Sea, they landed routinely at Anadyr. Refueled, the seaplanes then were flown to Magadan, located on the north coast of the Sea of Okhotsk. The Soviet airmen were returned via the ALSIB route to Fairbanks where U.S. Navy air transports were waiting to carry them back to Kodiak.

The Lend-Lease seaplanes, after delivery to Magadan, were scheduled for use in the Vladivostok area, and the Soviets planned to move them from Magadan before the Sea of Okhotsk began to freeze. By means of the air crew shuttle service, the Soviets successfully ferried all thirty seaplanes in small groups from Kodiak to Magadan in time to meet their self-imposed deadline of September 15.[28]

The Allied bargaining at Moscow in October and at Yalta four months later did not change the volume of Lend-Lease aircraft moving through Alaska as committed in the Fourth Protocol. From the beginning of the ALSIB route, some of the airplanes entering Siberia never arrived at the end of the route (Krasnoyarsk), where normally they would have been deployed to the German front. A few of the missing craft simply vanished somewhere in the wilderness along the ALSIB route. Others, however, were deliberately diverted, probably after having reached Yakutsk, to the Soviet Far Eastern front.

Since 1942, three air armies—the 9th, 10th, and 12th—had been based in the Soviet Far East to bolster the Soviet defenses against Japanese intrusion.[29] Now, as a result of Stalin's commitment at Yalta to enter the war with Japan, literally hundreds of Fourth Protocol fighters and bombers also were being diverted to the Soviet Far East for positioning and use (chap. 10).

American and Soviet collaboration to prepare for the Soviet Union's entry in the war faced indeterminate delays. Since Roosevelt had agreed to provide Lend-Lease items to the Soviet stockpile in Siberia, the United States was honoring its commitment. The Red Army operations planned against the Kwantung Army in Manchuria and in North China were exclusively Soviet, and planners from the U.S. Joint Chiefs of Staff were not involved. However, the preparation of American bases on Kamchatka and in the Maritime Provinces was a different matter. Joint Soviet-American base surveys were needed, but the Kremlin stalled. Eventually, the Joint Chiefs of Staff concluded that U.S. bases in the Soviet Far East were not essential to the conduct of American operations against the Japanese home islands. Instead, they decided to wait for the Soviets to consider whether it was in the Soviet Union's interest to undertake joint planning seriously for the preparation and use of American bases on the Asian mainland.[30]

In early April, 1945, Roosevelt remained both disappointed and disturbed by Stalin's uncooperative attitude with regard to the fulfillment of the joint planning pledges made at Moscow and Yalta. Preparations were well under way for the San Francisco Conference, and Roosevelt was also troubled by Stalin's refusal to send Molotov to the history-making world event. He pointed out to Stalin that the foreign affairs ministers of the other United Nations sponsoring powers and most of the other founding nations were pledged to attend.[31]

Without warning, the I&I Russian section in Alaska soon was deeply involved in the organizational web of the San Francisco Conference. In March, Lieutenant Chavchavadze was informed that he was eligible for a rest and recreation leave. Although he had been in Alaskan military service for only eighteen months, he did not dispute the opportunity. He departed for Washington and New York and did not return until May.[32] In April, Captain Gavrisheff was reassigned to the War Department General Staff (G-2). Capt. Eugene de Moore, having been requisitioned as Gavrisheff's replacement, arrived only a few days before Gavrisheff's departure.

In the midst of the turmoil in the command structure of the I&I Russian section, the liaison organization was informed to expect the arrival of several transport-loads of Soviet diplomatic delegations bound for San Francisco. The I&I section was ordered to provide a Russian-speaking escort to accompany each Soviet aircraft from Fairbanks to San Francisco and back.

Gavrisheff and Chavchavadze were gone and de Moore lacked experience in the Soviet-American liaison program. Therefore, the only remaining experienced officer, Captain Gubert from Nome, together with skillful noncommissioned interpreters from both Nome and Fairbanks, undertook the task of fulfilling the diplomatic escort mission.[33]

The first transport from Moscow to arrive at Fairbanks carried the Soviet secretariat group to make preparations at San Francisco for the various Soviet delegations that were following. Gubert, designated as the secretariat group's escort, joined the group during a rest stop at Fairbanks on April 11. "I shall always remember the day we landed at San Francisco," he said. "It was April the twelfth—the day that President Roosevelt died."[34]

In Moscow, Ambassador Harriman used the death of Roosevelt as an opportunity to persuade Stalin that he should change his mind and send Foreign Minister Molotov to San Francisco. He told Stalin that the most effective way to express the Soviet government's desire to continue collaboration with the United States was the presence of Molotov in Washington and San Francisco at this time. Although expressing his belief that American policy under President Truman would remain unchanged, Stalin agreed to Molotov's trip.[35]

Molotov arrived at Fairbanks on a special diplomatic transport en route to Washington on April 19. Since Gubert had not yet returned from San Francisco, Captain de Moore selected one of the I&I Russian section's senior noncommissioned officers—Sgt. Ilya Wolston—to serve as Molotov's escort. Following Molotov's arrival in Washington, he made his confrontation visit with President Truman on April 22 and then flew to San Francisco. The international conference convened on April 25 as planned.

Meanwhile, because Gubert had lived in the San Francisco area on the eve of the war, his familiarity with the city was an asset. He was instructed to escort members of the Soviet secretariat group around the city and "keep them out of trouble," Gubert said. "This was quite a challenge. You know how the Russians like to drink!"

In all, nine additional transports delivered Soviet diplomatic delegations before and during the conference. To eight of the transports, the following I&I escort/interpreters were assigned: Sergeants Tumarin, Gmirkin, Postovsky, and Chelnov from Nome and Sergeants Pekarsky, Remy, Rankov, and Levitsky from Fairbanks.

Being on the ground when the eight transports with their I&I escorts arrived at San Francisco, Gubert was able to correlate the duties of the escorts regarding their Soviet charges. "Most of the Soviet aircraft crews were from the ALSIB route and were well known to me and my interpreters," Gubert said. "Because they were disciplined to acceptable social behavior at Nome and Fairbanks, the ALSIB airmen were available to dampen any misbehavior by fellow Soviets. Fortunately, there were no unpleasant incidents or major problems during the conference," Gubert reported.[36]

The ninth Soviet transport carried two special delegations—the foreign ministers of the Ukrainian Republic and the Byelorussian Republic and their staffs. Gubert himself was ordered to Nome in late April to meet the incoming delegations, and he delivered them a few days later to the San Francisco Conference.[37]

Gubert was elated with his temporary assignment in San Francisco for good reason. After serving continuously for more than two years in

Alaska, he was able to stay with his wife and meet, for the first time, his daughter Natasha, who was born in 1943. "It was a wonderful break for me," he said.[38]

The San Francisco Conference, having accomplished the task of producing the charter for the United Nations Organization, was officially concluded on June 26. Each I&I escort returned to Alaska as the Soviet transports, one after another, carried the Soviet delegates and their staff personnel to the Soviet Union via the ALSIB route.

10.
Disconnection, Again

While ALSIB route personnel, both American and Soviet, must have sensed that their cooperative efforts were drawing to a close, they nonetheless were caught up in the climatic 1945 events that came thick and fast.

To the bustling Lend-Lease aerial ferrying operation were assigned two Soviet major generals to assume high positions on the ALSIB route in Alaska and Siberia.

One was Maj. Gen. Ivan A. Obrazkov, who came to Fairbanks in the winter of 1944–45.[1] Heretofore, the senior military official in Alaska had held the rank of colonel, a rank commensurate with that of the ATC Ladd Field commander but junior to Brigadier General Gaffney, commander of the ATC Alaskan Division. However, if General Obrazkov's presence created any awkwardness in Soviet-American relations at Ladd Field, it was not reflected in the uninterrupted Lend-Lease transfer operations there.

The other was Maj. Gen. Mark Shevelev, who replaced Col. Ilya Mazuruk as commander of the 1st Ferrying Aviation Division.[2] Like Mazuruk, who had developed the 3,500-mile ALSIB route across Siberia to Krasnoyarsk, General Shevelev was a polar aviation veteran and specialist.

The historic 1941 Alaska-Siberian aerial reconnection was of course the result of the twentieth-century invention of the airplane. However, harking back to the original intercontinental linkage by sea two hundred years earlier and responding to the needs of modern warfare, an Alaska-Siberian Lend-Lease sea route also secretly and belatedly became operational in late March, 1945, to deliver navy vessels to the Soviet Union. The route's American transfer base was at Cold Bay at the end of the Alaskan Peninsula. There, Soviet crewmen were trained to operate the navy craft before they sailed the vessels to Kamchatka and other Soviet Far Eastern navy bases.

During World War II, Lend-Lease agreements not only provided 125 cargo freighters (used primarily on the vital trans-Pacific supply artery that brushed the Aleutian Islands en route to Vladivostok) but a total of 556 navy vessels to the Soviets as well.[3] No capital ships were included in the program. Most of those transferred were frigates, submarine chasers, mine sweepers, landing craft, and similar small vessels.

Of the total of 556 Lend-Lease navy vessels, more than one-fourth were delivered to Soviet crews at Cold Bay. In the navy project referred to as Hula Two, the transfers of 149 craft began soon after the Yalta Conference. When satisfied that they were familiar with the operation of the ships, including thirty landing craft, Soviet Navy crews took the vessels in small flotillas to their Siberian bases. In all, 12,400 Soviet sailors were trained to man the vessels. Following V-J Day, the Hula Two project ended on September 5 and the last Soviet departed Cold Bay three weeks later, on September 29. The Cold Bay base itself was permanently closed on December 1, 1945.[4]

Meanwhile, in late April, 1945, while the San Francisco Conference was being assembled, American and Soviet negotiators in Washington had begun the process of determining what kind of Lend-Lease support might be included in a Fifth Protocol. The Lend-Lease provisions contained in the Fourth Protocol were due to expire on June 30.

A new protocol was never reached. American official reaction to the May 8 German surrender was swift. On May 12, orders were flashed to cease any further Lend-Lease shipments and deliveries to the Soviet Union. The abrupt action caused a diplomatic storm in Moscow.[5] The Soviets bitterly resented the unilateral U.S. announcement, issued without any warning to or consultation with the Soviet Union. The bitterness lingered, adding fuel to resurfacing Soviet suspicion of American policies.

American envoys rushed to assure Stalin that the orders pertained only to Lend-Lease deliveries for use in the war with Germany. They emphasized that the Lend-Lease supplies for use in the Far East against Japan would be forthcoming as promised. In light of the uncertainty regarding the role that the Soviets would play in the war against Japan, it was decided that the balance of the aircraft commitments under the Fourth Protocol would be supplied.[6]

Following the Soviet acceptance of the remedied P-63 fighters and the recovery of the ALSIB route from its paralysis in November, 1944, the flow of Lend-Lease aircraft resumed its breakneck pace.[7] An average of 270 planes passed through Fairbanks each month during the November, 1944-June, 1945, period. This remarkable rate was maintained despite the severe winter weather conditions and the mid-May confusion caused by the delivery stop order from Washington.

During the winter and spring, the Soviets accepted not only P-63 fighters but B-25 bombers and C-47 transports as well. In addition, the Soviets made special requests for two-engine and single-engine trainers. After being advised that the two-engine trainers were not available, the Soviets agreed to accept A-20 bombers as substitute training craft. The single-engine AT6-F trainers were available, and delivery of both A-20s and AT6-Fs commenced in May.[8]

On June 25, 1945, Valeri Minakov and his son Oleg reached the Eskimo village of Savoonga on St. Lawrence Island, the largest U.S. island possession in the northern Bering Sea. The thirty-six-year-old father and six-year-old son had pulled off a harrowing escape from the nearby Siberian coast in a motor-driven, skin-covered kayak: this unlikely pair were the only known successful Soviet defectors from Siberia to Alaska since the Red Revolution.[9]

A skilled marine motor mechanic, Minakov had been sent to Provid/eniya Bay on the southeastern tip of the Chukotski Peninsula in early 1944. After his wife deserted him and Oleg in mid-1944, Minakov began to plan his escape to Alaska. During the following year he built a small kayak ten feet long, fabricated a rudder attachment from a bicycle frame, and hoarded containers of fuel for his outboard motor.

Finally, on June 23, 1945, he was ready. He had earlier informed the local NKVD office of his intention to visit a small nearby island for bird egg hunting, a common local practice. Shortly after 4:00 A.M., Minakov and his son rowed the kayak between masses of floating ice near Cape Chaplino. He then started his outboard motor and set a course for Alaska, aiming for the mouth of the Yukon River. Minakov suspected that his escape would be discovered once the NKVD officials realized that he had not returned from his egg-hunting trip. He also assumed, despite the Bering Sea's turbulent weather and the ever-present ice floes, that a sea search for his kayak was inevitable.

His voyage suddenly became more hazardous when there was an unexpected drop in temperature. Thin ice began to form between the heavier ice floes. As the outboard motor drove the kayak through the thickening, frigid water, Minakov was concerned that the sharp icy particles might puncture the kayak's thin walrus hide cover.

Sometime on June 24, Minakov sighted a sailing vessel approaching from the Siberian coast. To lighten his kayak, he threw his extra containers of fuel overboard. The weather worsened. Fortunately, a blanket of fog rose to cover the sea, and the kayak was hidden from the pursuers. Without his spare fuel, Minakov abandoned his plan to reach the mouth of the Yukon River. Instead, he veered south toward St. Lawrence Island, to land at Savoonga on the island's north shore.

When the sea became calmer, Minakov and Oleg moved in the kayak to the Eskimo village of Gambell on the northwestern edge of the island. Gambell was closer to Siberia, which made Minakov uneasy. But Gambell had the advantage of reliable communication service with the Alaskan mainland. During the ensuing two-week period while father and son waited to be officially evacuated from the island, they had an unwelcome visitor: a small Soviet warship dropped anchor near the village and the Minakovs went into hiding.[10] However, the vessel later hoisted anchor and disappeared, and on July 11, Valeri and Oleg Minakov were flown from Gambell via Anchorage to Seattle.

A week later, on July 18, a Soviet fishing ketch anchored near Gambell. This time, fourteen Siberian Eskimos came ashore "to visit with Gambell's families." Some of the Gambell elders had actually been born in villages on the opposite Siberian coast and still had blood relatives there. In past years when conditions were favorable, illegal exchange visits between relatives had been made across the sea. The Gambell villagers, however, were convinced that the real reason for this visit was to search for Minakov's trail. Why else, the villagers asked, would the Siberians inquire whether they had seen "a white Russian"?[11] After two days, the visitors returned to their ketch without a positive answer. The Minakov trail apparently was successfully hidden from the Soviet hunters, at least temporarily.

Although a mere flyspeck in the history of the Alaska-Siberian connection, the Minakov incident was indicator that foretold a return of rising Soviet-American tensions.

During the last weeks of July, the final Big Three summit of the war was held at Potsdam on the outskirts of Berlin's rubble. The conference mainly addressed European problems, but the situation in the Far East was not ignored. One of the first agreements was to issue the Allies' "unconditional surrender" ultimatum to Japan. President Harry S. Truman, after being informed of the successful testing of the atomic bomb in New Mexico, told Stalin on July 24 that "we have a new weapon of unusual destructive power." Stalin reacted by commenting that "he hoped we would make good use of it against the Japanese."[12]

Thirteen days later, in the early morning hours of August 6, the people of the Japanese city of Hiroshima were only casually aware of the lone American B-29 bomber high above them. Seconds later, in one deadly historic blast, an atomic bomb destroyed the city and thousands of people.

Stalin kept his promise and the Soviet Union entered the war against Japan on schedule. Red Army divisions surged across the Soviet-Manchurian border on August 8, exactly three months following the German surrender. The Japanese border defenses were quickly penetrated. The remnants of the Kuantung Army, once so feared, offered no effective resistance, and the Red Army rolled rapidly southward.

Even as the Japanese defenders were being overwhelmed, White Russian paramilitary settlements in the border area were captured by Red Army paratroopers on the first day. As though well rehearsed, the Red Army promptly put an end to the smoldering twenty-seven-year-old war between the White Russians and the Bolsheviks dating from 1918. From the village commanded by Col. Anatole Madievsky, all of the men were marched to a field, ordered to dig their own common grave, and then were summarily executed. The same fate awaited many of the survivors from other White Russian paramilitary frontier villages. So died Colonel Madievsky, the father-in-law of Capt. Igor Gubert, recently returned to his American duty station at Nome following his assignment to escort Soviet dignitaries to and at the San Francisco Conference.[13]

After a second atomic bomb was dropped on the port and city of Nagasaki, the Japanese government accepted the Allies' terms for surrender on August 14. On the same day, the signing of a Sino-Soviet treaty in Moscow returned to the Soviet Union lost Russian privileges in Manchuria, including rights in the Chinese cities of Dairen and Port Arthur.[14]

However, not until August 18 did an invasion fleet from Kamchatka carry Red Army troops to seize and occupy the Kurile Islands. The Japanese resisted fiercely on Shumushu, the northern-most island, before surrendering on August 23. Japanese defenses on other key Kurile Islands later also collapsed.[15]

Lend-Lease aircraft delivered to the Soviets at Fairbanks in July numbered 157, representing most of the remaining commitments in the Lend-Lease aircraft pipeline. Half of the planes were P-63 fighters, the remainder being A-20 bombers (substitutes for trainers) and C-47 transports.

In August, another thirty-seven airplanes—two P-63s, two A-20s, and thirty-three C-47s—were ferried to Fairbanks. Originally, all of them were earmarked for release to the Soviets. However, following Japan's surrender, Washington decided to cease Lend-Lease deliveries on September 2 (V-J Day). Seventeen were transferred to the Soviets in time to meet the September 2 deadline, but the remaining twenty, all C-47 transports, were ordered to be grounded at Fairbanks. After a delay of several weeks, the transports were transferred to the Alaskan Department for its Troop Carrier Command.[16]

Once the last of the seventeen red-starred aircraft winged across the Bering Sea, the ALSIB ferrying program came to its end. The Alaska-Siberian connection by air was made possible as a wartime necessity and, despite both natural and political obstacles, the operation of the ALSIB route was recognized as a major Soviet-American achievement.

During the short life span of the ALSIB ferrying operation, the Soviets accepted 7,924 Lend-Lease fighters, bombers, and transports at Fairbanks (appendix A).[17] According to Soviet records, seventy-three of these airplanes were lost on the ALSIB route between Fairbanks and Krasnoyarsk (chap. 6).

Of the remaining 7,851 airplanes, 543 never reached the end of the ALSIB route at Krasnoyarsk. Instead, after Germany surrendered, aircraft in the Lend-Lease pipeline were diverted from the route in Siberia and assigned to the Red Air Force in in the Soviet Far East.[18]

In all during 1942–45, a total of 7,308 airplanes completed the flight from Fairbanks to Krasnoyarsk,[19] where they were made available for combat, training, or transport duty.

Beginning in late August, the Soviet presence at Fairbanks and Nome steadily dwindled. In early September, the last few Lend-Lease airplanes were crossing Siberia, and their journey heralded the imminent departure of the last Soviets.

At the same time, the numbers of ATC personnel involved in the ferrying operation in Alaska were rapidly reduced. New commanders had recently been assigned at Nome's Marks Field (Col. James H. Potter) and at Ladd Field (Col. Louis M. Merrick), but they inherited doomed commands.

The I&I Russian section's commander, the recently promoted Major de Moore, flew to Nome to assist Igor Gubert in closing the I&I liaison outpost at Moses Point. A steady stream of I&I section interpreters at both Fairbanks and Nome were returning to the continental United States for reassignment or release from active duty. As October arrived, only

Some of the last group of Soviet personnel at Fairbanks before departing for their return to the Soviet Union on October 9, 1945. Bidding them farewell were American liaison officers Lieutenant Chavchavadze, *left*, and Major de Moore, *second from right*. Courtesy David Chavchavadze

a handful of liaison personnel remained, including the three officers—de Moore and Chavchavadze at Fairbanks and Gubert at Nome. The Soviet presence at Fairbanks was down to bare bones, and the last Soviet had already departed from Nome. At Fairbanks, Sgt. Nicholas P. Tiurin was assigned to pack the Soviet Military Mission's remaining equipment for shipment to the Soviet Union.[20]

Unexpectedly, on October 7, a Soviet transport bearing twenty-four Soviet Navy officers and seamen from the Soviet Baltic Fleet reached Fairbanks from Moscow. Because the navy group was ahead of schedule for schooling at a coast guard installation at Groton, Connecticut, the group's Washington sponsors ordered the Ladd Field authorities to hold the men in Alaska until further notice. David Chavchavadze noted the boredom of the marooned seamen and, since he himself was likewise idle, privately initiated a program of activities to entertain them.[21]

On October 9, the last ten personnel of the "Russian colony" in Alaska were ready to leave. Both de Moore and Chavchavadze escorted them to their waiting transport, where the ranking members of the party—a civilian comptroller, three senior military officers (one with wife and child), and an NKVD officer—posed for an obligatory farewell photograph.[22] Almost immediately, the transport was airborne and rose higher and higher in the western sky where Siberia beckoned. The sight and sound of the fading airplane marked the symbolic conclusion to the unique Alaska-Siberian air connection wrought by means of the Lend-Lease program.

Two weeks later, Washington finally ordered the stranded Soviet Navy group to resume its journey to the coast guard school. Chavchavadze volunteered to escort them. De Moore agreed because he assumed that Chavchavadze would return.[23] However, Chavchavadze knew that he, like the recently departed Soviets, was taking his final leave of Alaska.

His liaison responsibilities at Nome having ceased, Igor Gubert closed his office, conferred with de Moore at Ladd Field, went to Alaskan Department headquarters at Fort Richardson to write his final report, and departed Alaska on November 21 to be released from active duty.[24] With the exception of two enlisted interpreters, Major de Moore's command had vanished. His I&I Russian section was soon deactivated.

And so, Ladd Field's wartime key mission of supporting the international Lend-Lease ferrying mission was over. On November 2, operational control of Ladd Field—where the Northwest route merged with the ALSIB route—passed from the Air Transport Command to the Eleventh Air Force (later the Alaskan Air Command).[25] Ladd Field's wartime satellite base, Mile 26, was later expanded and developed into Eielson Air Force Base which, together with Elmendorf Air Force Base, provided the backbone of Alaska's air defenses during the Cold War. In 1961, the former Ladd Field was transferred to the U.S. Army and designated as Fort Wainwright, where a portion of the army ground forces in Alaska was garrisoned.[26]

The wartime reconnection of Alaska with Siberia was not yet completely severed, but military and political suspicions, having been carefully suppressed by the Soviet-American mutual need for insuring the defeat of Germany and Japan, simmered anew once the battlefields were quiet. The Cold War loomed ahead. Because of its mounting intensity, Alaska and Siberia would again be disconnected, this time for nearly a half-century.

Postscript

Among the key figures in the ALSIB route story, several went on to further military and government service.[1] The route itself has been back in the news occasionally, notably during worldwide fiftieth anniversary ceremonies commemorating World War II events. And the connections between Siberia and Alaska are growing closer than they have been at any time since the end of the Lend-Lease aircraft deliveries.

George Kisevalter, following reassignment to Washington in 1944, devoted the next year to duty with the War Department General Staff (G-2). When Germany surrendered in 1945, Kisevalter went to Europe to debrief senior German intelligence officials on their knowledge of the Soviet armed forces. He decided to leave active military service in 1946 and return to some aspect of his chosen professional field of engineering. Electing to settle in Nebraska, he designed and built factories to dehydrate and grind freshly cut alfalfa into meal for use as poultry feed. Later he became manager of three factories, two in Nebraska and one in Kansas.

In 1951, the new Central Intelligence Agency (CIA) sought to recruit him. Following discussions in Washington, he agreed to become a Soviet operations branch chief and quickly was involved in intelligence activities in the Far East. For nearly two years he traveled in Korea, Japan, and Hong Kong.

Beginning in 1953, Kisevalter's Soviet operational attention was switched to Europe. For the next nine years he participated in sensitive intelligence operations in Vienna, Berlin, London, and Paris. Meanwhile, he was steadily promoted within the CIA and reached super-grade rank in 1963. He also kept his army reserve commission in good standing.

During his remaining years with the CIA, he made official trips of short duration to Ankara, Mexico City, Ottawa, Montreal, Copenhagen, and Geneva. Kisevalter reached the agency's mandatory retirement age in 1970 after a brilliant career, during which he was awarded the Distinguished Intelligence Medal and the agency's Certificate of Merit and Distinction. He retired from the army reserves with the rank of colonel. He and his wife reared one daughter. His wife is deceased.

When Michael Gavrisheff departed Alaska in 1945 for anticipated duty with the War Department General Staff, his arrival in Washington coincided with the end of the war in Europe. His services no longer needed in the Pentagon, he was promptly rerouted to Berlin. He wound up with staff duty in the Four Power deliberations, first in the interpreters' pool, then as a secretary in the agriculture division and later in the transportation division, and finally as the executive secretary of the German External Property Commission.

In 1947, Gavrisheff returned to the United States for counterintelligence schooling, followed by duty in New York City. A year later, he became chief of the Russian language section in the Army Counterintelligence Center at Fort Holabird, Maryland.

Leaving active military service as an army reserve major in 1949, Gavrisheff started a civilian career at the Library of Congress as a research analyst of materials related to the Soviet Union. He also studied toward an advanced degree in international relations in Washington and, during a leave of absence, in Mexico City. In 1960, he resigned his position with the Library of Congress to become involved in political fundraising activities, and a series of entrepreneurships followed. In the meantime, he married and fathered a son and two daughters, one of whom is deceased. Michael Gavrisheff and his wife are the owners and operators of a word-processing and desktop publishing company.

Igor Gubert returned to San Francisco to rejoin his wife Alla and their daughter as an appropriate homecoming day approached—Thanksgiving, 1945. Following holiday leave, Gubert was released from active military service with an appointment as an army reserve major. He was recalled to active duty briefly in 1951 during the Korean War mobilization and served at the Army Language School in Monterey, California. When his army commission expired in 1953, he did not renew it.

In the meantime, Gubert went through an adjustment period and then settled into his professional life. He became a successful building contractor and owned and managed real estate properties. "My wife Alla,

my son Alex (born 1946) and daughter Natasha are my business part-
ners and my helpers," he said proudly. "They are also my best friends."
He added, "[I am] the immigrant kid in America—making good beyond
his wildest dreams. Thank you, America, my new Motherland!"[2]

Gubert's mother, who survived World War II in the White Russian
refugee colony in Shanghai, was able to immigrate to the United States
in 1947 to be near her son and his family for the rest of her life. She died
in 1986 at the age of ninety-five. Alla's mother, widowed by Colonel Madievsky's 1945 execution in Manchuria, lived in the San Francisco area
until her death in 1978.

Having finally delivered his Soviet Baltic Fleet seamen to Groton, Connecticut, David Chavchavadze was temporarily assigned to a German
prisoner of war camp near Fort Story, Virginia. When he later was assigned to duty in Germany, he was promptly attached to the American
liaison and protocol section of the Allied Secretariat of the Allied Control Authority. During his Berlin tour of duty, he found three of his wartime colleagues from Alaska: Capt. Michael Gavrisheff, Lt. Paul Duncan,
and Ilya Wolston, the latter a civilian employee of a commercial airline.

Chavchavadze returned to the United States for release from active
military service in 1947, at which time he was promoted to army reserve
captain. He reentered Yale University to complete the education interrupted by World War II. Following graduation in 1950, he joined the CIA
to continue patriotic service for his adopted country—service that endured for the next quarter-century. He completed a long overseas tour
of duty in Germany and another in South America and made official
visits to various countries on every continent except Australia. During
his CIA career he also was promoted to army reserve major.

After retirement from the CIA in 1974, he waited two years and then
successfully applied for a Soviet visa to visit the ancestral land that he
had never seen. That first visit to Moscow and Leningrad (St. Petersburg) in 1976 opened the door for him to revisit the Soviet Union during his retirement years. David Chavchavadze has authored several
successful books, all bearing on Russian history and Soviet activities.
He is the father of three daughters and a son.

Both Col. Ilya Mazuruk and Col. Michael Machin received their nation's highest award—Hero of the Soviet Union—after leaving the ALSIB
route ferrying operations. Before they retired, they gained general officer
status—Mazuruk major general and Machin lieutenant general. Mazuruk is deceased. Machin lives in Moscow, where ALSIB route veterans
helped him celebrate his eighty-fifth birthday in 1992.

Elena Makarova kept her promise to marry Peter Gamov. They were wed in 1950. Once he had been demobilized, Gamov began a career in civil aviation as an Aeroflot pilot, and Makarova became a senior instructor of technical translation at the Zukossky Military Engineering Aircraft Academy. Among her students were the first Soviet cosmonauts, including Yury Gagarin and Titov. She was awarded a cosmonaut medal by the USSR Federation of Cosmonauts when she retired after twenty-three years of service. Their son, Valeriy, also an Aeroflot pilot, was assigned to routes in the Russian Far East. Both Gamov and Makarova were actively involved in the organized activities of the Soviet War Veterans Committee in Moscow, with Makarova acting as secretary of the ALSIB veterans section. They died unexpectedly in Moscow, Gamov in June, 1995, and Makarova in October, 1995.

Natasha Fenelonova, who served in Alaska with Makarova, continued to be her close friend for over fifty years. After the war, Fenelonova worked for many years at scientific institutions as an interpreter/translator. In her retirement years she has been in declining health due to the ravages of Parkinson's disease. Her husband, Nicholas Tiurin, whom she married at Fairbanks, was graduated from the Aviation Institute and is a senior aviation engineer. They are the parents of a daughter and live in Moscow.

The Valeri Minakov story did not end happily. Following his daring escape from Siberia across the Bering Sea to St. Lawrence Island in 1945, Minakov and his son Oleg settled in Washington state. Within a few years, however, Minakov feared that his identity and location had been discovered and he reported that he was being harassed. Whether the harassment was imaginary or real was never confirmed, but some of his friends believed that the long arm of Soviet intelligence agents was responsible. Minakov developed mental illness so severe that he spent the rest of his life in a hospital; he died in 1967. His son went on to live his own life, apparently without further fear.[3]

The ALSIB route was to return to the public eye a few times during the Cold War years. In 1949, Maj. George R. Jordan, an ATC liaison officer at Great Falls during the war, charged that various U.S. government officials had aided and abetted Soviet espionage by allowing the export of atomic materials and tons of classified documents over the ALSIB Lend-Lease route to the Soviet Union.[4]

Jordan's sensational charges were made in interviews by Fulton Lewis, Jr., on nationwide radio broadcasts and in a later book, *From Major Jordan's Diaries*.[5] He also testified before the congressional Joint Committee on Atomic Energy. The committee's investigation concluded that (1) there was no basis for Jordan's charges against the accused governmental officials, (2) there were no indications that unauthorized documents were smuggled via the ALSIB route, and (3) small amounts of uranium-related materials were shipped from the United States to the Soviet Union with the knowledge and consent of the U.S. government.[6]

Jordan's 1952 book, however, was well received. It was reprinted in four subsequent editions in 1958, 1961, 1965, and 1984. The last edition was dedicated to the memory of Congressman Lawrence P. McDonald who, along with 268 other passengers and crewmen, died when a Red Air Force fighter destroyed the Korean Air Lines (KAL) flight 007 aircraft over Sakhalin Island in 1983.

At least one of the remote airfields that was hastily built across Siberia in 1942 on the ALSIB route apparently has remained in use. Silvio ("Scotty") Sclocchini was a retired American army command sergeant major who lived in Irkutsk, Siberia, with his wife, a native Siberian. Because of an interest in the history of the ALSIB route, Sclocchini sought additional information regarding the wartime activity and was referred to the author. "In 1988," he wrote, "we flew to Bilibino in the Siberian Far North to visit my wife's family. On our way, our small plane landed at Seymchan [a base on the wartime ALSIB route]. It looked strangely familiar and I felt that I had been there before."[7]

Vladimir Metelitea, a Soviet reporter at Bilibino, later told Sclocchini that the Seymchan airfield had been built by U.S. military engineers. Seymchan's metal mat runway was the original one, Metelitea said. Before his death in 1990, Sclocchini was persuaded that since American army engineers were prohibited from entering Siberia, the Soviets themselves may have improved the runway with metal mats obtained through Lend-Lease.

Thomas J. Watson, Jr., who in 1942 had accompanied General Bradley to Moscow to organize the ALSIB route, was U.S. ambassador to the Soviet Union from 1979 to 1981. In 1987, the retired international businessman gained permission to fly his private jet aircraft from Moscow across Siberia to Alaska over the former ALSIB route. Obtaining the Soviet Union's consent marked a crack in the conduct of the Cold War.

Until this crack occurred, the Soviet veterans of the ALSIB route had had no official status. As a result of Watson's feat, the Soviet War Veterans Committee recognized the historical significance of the wartime ALSIB cooperative achievement. Once the ALSIB veterans were officially recognized, they immediately began to plan a Soviet-American reunion.

In April, 1988, eight Soviet veterans banded together and placed an open letter in the magazine *Soviet Life*, published for American readers. Among the signatories of the letter were Generals Mazuruk, Machin, and Shevelev as well as Captains Peter Gamov, Victor Perov, and David Sherl, all prominent personalities in the history of the ALSIB route. The letter contained both a plea for peace and an invitation: "Let's meet again!" in Alaska.[8]

The appeal for a reunion quickly brought results. In late May, 1990, an entourage of twenty-seven Soviet veterans plus Soviet officials and media representatives were welcomed to Nome, Fairbanks, and Anchorage. Two years later, in July of 1992, a similar group including thirty-eight veterans came to Fairbanks to attend an ALSIB Lend-Lease symposium and a fiftieth anniversary celebration of the ALSIB route's founding.

In the 1980s, the Soviet ALSIB route veterans' efforts leading to recognition coincidentally sparked interest in the discovery of wrecks of Lend-Lease aircraft that had vanished on remote sections of the ALSIB route across Siberia. When wreckage was discovered, the remains of dead crewmen were recovered, identified, and buried with military honors, usually in cemeteries containing the bodies of other fallen military airmen.

As the search for additional wrecks in the Siberian wilderness has continued, monuments have been erected at points along the wartime ferry route, including at Kirensk, Seymchan, and at Egvekinot, a village near Uel'kal.

Victor Perov, an ALSIB route veteran, has reported that "Uel'kal is now in a remote region on the coast and the former air base has been destroyed. No plane can land there." After the war ended, Perov became a well-known polar aviator and often visited landing fields on the former ferry route. "The small village of Uel'kal is now very difficult to reach," he said. "Some years ago, the villagers asked me to identify the dead pilots buried in the cemetery, but I could not remember their names." Since Egvekinot had a landing field, the Uel'kal memorial monument was located there. Perov and two other ALSIB ferry route veterans attended ceremonies dedicating monument.[9]

Another major monument to commemorate the achievements of the ALSIB route pilots was formally dedicated at Yakutsk in October, 1992. The Soviet veterans have suggested that an appropriate memorial to Soviet-American wartime aviation collaboration be erected at Fairbanks, Nome, or both.

In 1986, plans were being germinated for celebrating the approaching 250th anniversary of the Russian discovery of Alaska, and the likelihood of an Alaska-Siberian reconnection seemed possible. Two years later in 1988, *glasnost* cracked the Siberian coastal barrier long main-

ALSIB reunion in Alaska, 1990. *Front row, left to right:* Peter P. Gamov, bomber squadron commander and leader of fighters; Vladimir I. Souvorov, fighter pilot; Fedor A. Zhevlakov, fiighter squadron commander. *Back row, left to right:* Victor Elsukov, transport radio operator; Ivan Moiseev, pilot of transport that brought original Soviet Military Mission to Alaska, 1942; Victor Perov, fighter pilot. Courtesy Elena Makarova

tained during the Cold War, and Soviet officials agreed to a one-day good-will visit by Alaskans from Nome to Provideniya on the tip of the Chu-kotski Peninsula. A U.S. airliner with eighty Eskimos, politicians, peace advocates, and journalists was warmly greeted when the plane landed at Provideniya on June 14.

By this time, the Bering Sea thaw had become obvious. The active Soviet-American joint planning for celebrating Bering's voyage foresaw many events in and visits to Sitka, Kodiak, Cordova, and Unalaska (Dutch Harbor), all in Alaska, as well as at Petropavlovsk, Bering's Siberian base.

The climatic event of the celebration involved Vitus Bering himself. In 1741 after he had sighted the Alaskan mainland, his ship, the *St. Peter*, was storm-wrecked in the Komandorski Islands on its return voyage to Petropavlovsk. Ill and weak, Bering died. Two hundred and fifty years later in 1991, Danish archeologists uncovered the graves of several of the crewmen and discovered Bering's skeletal remains. After intensive study of the remains at the Institute of Forensic Medicine in Moscow, forensic physician Victor N. Zviagin constructed a facial image of the famous explorer.[10]

On September 14, 1992, Bering's remains were ceremoniously rein-terred in the Komandorskis on Bering Island, south of the Bering Strait in the Bering Sea.

The crumbling of the Cold War barriers dividing Alaska from Siberia accelerated so much that in mid-September, 1990, Aeroflot made its first ever commercial flight from Khabarovsk to Anchorage and return. Stem-ming from this breakthrough, the U.S. Department of Transportation announced in December that a new air service agreement with the So-viet Union had been reached. Alaska Airlines was awarded a passenger route for regular nonstop service between Anchorage, Magadan, and Khabarovsk to begin in June, 1991. The inaugural flight from Anchor-age was the first of flights three times weekly during the summer months. Four years later, in 1995, Alaska Airlines commenced weekly summer flights between Seattle and Petropavlovsk via Anchorage. Aeroflot Rus-sian International Airlines also began weekly Anchorage-Magadan and Anchorage-Khabarovsk flight service year-round as well as regular polar service between Anchorage and Moscow/St. Petersburg.

Before World War II, aviation pioneers dreamed of unrestricted inter-national air service between Alaska and Siberia. Some of the dreams, of course, were obliquely fulfilled during the war when the temporary ALSIB Lend-Lease route became an operational success. A half-century passed before the dream of a permanent Alaska-Siberian connection by air re-alized at last.

The 1990s have brought other moves toward reconnection, too. In 1991, a century and a quarter after Russia had sold its Alaskan territory to the United States, the strident voice of a Russian ultranationalist presidential candidate, Vladimir Zhirinovsky, unexpectedly caught the attention of 7 percent of the Russian voters. He presented to them the vision of a restored Russian empire, including the repossession of Alaska. Again in 1993, Zhirinovsky's appeal to Russian nationalism caught fire and spread. In the newly elected parliament, nearly 25 percent of the delegates were from Zhirinovsky's Liberal Democratic Party.[11]

And then there is the railroad idea. A century after the project was first considered, the notion of connecting Alaska and Siberia by railroad tunnel under the Bering Strait refuses to die. In 1993, renewed interest in an intercontinental tunnel to join Eurasian and American railroads surfaced in Alaskan and Siberian governmental circles.[12]

An international transcontinental consortium, based in the United States, is interested in studying the project's economic feasibility as well as its technological requirements. Russian academic studies have reported that the cost of shipments from the United States to Asia by rail could be as much as 50 percent lower than by ship. The cost of the project has been variously estimated, the highest figure being $50 billion.[13]

The world is smaller today than it was when Vitus Bering first sighted the Alaskan shore or when ALSIB route pilots struggled to ferry their airplanes through the hazards of northern frontier territory. Alaska and Siberia may yet see connection by land follow the pioneering efforts by sea and by air.

Notes

PREFACE

1. Hereafter referred to as the ALSIB route.
2. Robert H. Jones, *The Roads to Russia: United States Lend-Lease to the Soviet Union* (Norman: University of Oklahoma Press, 1969), 277.
3. Hereafter referred to as the Northwest route.
4. Otis Hays, Jr., "White Star, Red Star," *Alaska Journal* (Summer, 1982), 17.
5. Alaska Defense Command G-2 Russian Information Reports, Feb.–May, 1943, Record Group 407, National Archives (hereafter cited as G-2 Russian Report, with date).
6. Alaska Defense Command/Alaskan Department G-2 Weekly Reports, May, 1943–Nov. 1945, Record Group 338, National Archives (hereafter cited as G-2 Report no.,———annex,———with date).

CHAPTER 1

1. Ernest P. Walker, *Alaska: America's Continental Frontier Outpost* (Washington: Smithsonian Institution, 1943), 22–23.
2. Benson Bobrick, *East of the Sun* (New York: Poseidon Press, 1992), 40–47. Cossacks were independent frontiersmen, often including outlaws and adventurers, who staked out lives for themselves along the advancing fringes of the Russian empire in Siberia.
3. W. Bruce Lincoln, *Conquest of a Continent* (New York: Random House, 1994), 58–62.
4. Bobrick, *East of the Sun*, 67–72.
5. These *ostrogs* formed the nuclei for settlements and trade centers, most of which later developed into major Siberian cities. Among those that played significant roles in the history of the Alaska-Siberian connection were Krasnoyarsk (1628), Yakutsk (1632), and Irkutsk (1652). More than three hundred years later, Krasnoyarsk became the western terminal of

the Alaska-Siberian (ALSIB) air ferry route, Yakutsk became the middle relay point on the route, and Irkutsk was and still is the fur capital of Siberia.

6. Lincoln, *Conquest of a Continent*, 63.
7. Harry Schwartz, *Tsars, Mandarins and Commissars* (Garden City, N.Y.: Doubleday, 1973), 30.
8. Bobrick, *East of the Sun*, 96–97.
9. Stuart Ramsay Tompkins, *Alaska: Promyshlennik and Sourdough* (Norman: University of Oklahoma Press, 1945), 22–23.
10. Ibid., 25–27.
11. Richard A. Pierce, *Russian America: A Biographical Dictionary* (Kingston, Ont., Canada: Limestone Press, 1990), 120–21. Cape Dezhnev (East Cape) is named for the cossack Semen Dezhnev, who was a survivor of an ivory hunting expedition in 1648–49. He sailed from the Siberian Arctic coast east and south through the Bering Strait but did not glimpse the Alaskan coast. His forgotten report was later discovered in Yakutsk's archives in 1736.
12. Gerhard Friedrich Muller, *Bering's Voyages: The Reports from Russia* (Fairbanks: University of Alaska Press, 1986), 25–32.
13. L. A. Goldenberg and James L. Smith (ed.), *Gvozdev: The Russian Discovery of Alaska in 1732* (Anchorage: White Stone Press, 1990), 59–66. Meanwhile, also in 1732, a cossack expedition with Mikhail Gvozdev returned to the Bering Strait area where Gvozdev reported having observed the Alaskan coast.
14. Muller, *Bering's Voyages*, 96–99, 112–17.
15. Steve J. Langdon, *The Native People of Alaska* (Anchorage: Greatland Graphics, 1987), 12–13.
16. Rosa G. Liapunova, "Aleuts before Contact with the Russians: Some Demographic and Cultural Aspects," *Pacifica* (Nov., 1990), 9.
17. Mari Sardy, "Early Contact between Aleuts and Russians, 1741–1780," *Alaska History* (Fall–Winter, 1985), 43–52.
18. Langdon, *Native People of Alaska*, 21.
19. Grigorii I. Shelikhov, *A Voyage to America, 1783–1786* (Kingston, Ont., Canada: Limestone Press, 1981), 8–17.
20. Hector Chevigny, *Russian America: The Great Alaskan Venture, 1741–1867* (New York: Viking, 1965), 59–64.
21. Steven M. Peterson, "Russian Building Traditions and Their Legacy in Alaska," *Pacifica* (Nov., 1990), 131. Orthodox church influence in Alaska dates from the arrival of this first missionary group in 1794. Twenty-five years later, with Russian American Company support, Orthodox missions were planted among Aleut and Eskimo villages, where some ac-

tive Orthodox churches are still found. In 1979, thirty-seven of the churches were nominated for inclusion in the National Register of Historic Places because of their unique architecture.

22. Chevigny, *Great Alaskan Venture*, 70.
23. Ibid., 75.
24. Pierce, *Russian America*, 419.
25. Founded by Baranov and initially named New Archangel.
26. James R. Gibson, *Imperial Russia in Frontier America* (New York: Oxford University Press, 1976), 95–111.
27. Ibid., 154–58.
28. Ibid., 112–39. The colonists at Fort Ross were recalled in 1841 and Fort Ross was sold to John Sutter.
29. Historians and contemporary writers have referred either to "the manager of the Russian American Company" or to "the governor of Russian America." Both titles have been used to identify the same official designated as Russia's supreme authority in Alaska.
30. Chevigny, *Great Alaskan Venture*, 185.
31. Ibid., 205.
32. Lydia T. Black, "Creoles in Russian America," *Pacifica* (Nov., 1990), 142–53.
33. Pierce, *Russian America*, 371. Muraviev believed that a trans-Siberian railroad was essential to the growth of Russia's Far Eastern empire.
34. Chevigny, *Great Alaskan Venture*, 219–20.
35. William R. Hunt, *Arctic Passage* (New York: Scribner's, 1975), 111.
36. Bobrick, *East of the Sun*, 260–61.
37. David Hunter Miller, *The Alaska Treaty* (Kingston, Ont., Canada: Limestone Press, 1981), 38–39.
38. George Kennan, *Tent Life in Siberia* (Salt Lake City: Peregrine Smith Books, 1986), 1–2.
39. Phillip H. Ault, "The (Almost) Russian-American Telegraph," *American Heritage* (June, 1975), 92, 97.
40. Miller, *Alaska Treaty*, 1–2, 104–20.
41. Pierce, *Russian America*, 327–29.
42. Ibid., 158–59.
43. Ibid., 329–32.
44. The line was especially symbolic: in conjunction with the invisible political and cultural wedges that were being slipped between Alaska and Siberia, time itself cooperated.
45. Hunt, *Arctic Passage*, 262–78.
46. Bobrick, *East of the Sun*, 352–53.
47. Ibid., 353.

48. William H. Goetzmann and Kay Sloan, *Looking Far North* (New York: Viking, 1982), 127–28, 176–77, 196. In 1899, Edward Harriman sponsored and led a scientific expedition toward the Bering Strait. Harriman died in 1909 still convinced that a tunnel at the Bering Strait was the key to a global railroad system.

49. Terrence Cole, "The Bridge to Tomorrow," *Alaska History* (Fall, 1990), 8–11.

50. John J. Stephan, *The Kuril Islands: Russo-Japanese Frontier in the Pacific* (New York: Oxford University Press, 1974), 1.

51. The railroad theoretically was a joint Chinese-Russian venture but in fact was administered and controlled by Russia.

52. Bobrick, *East of the Sun*, 360–65; Lincoln, *Conquest of a Continent*, 244–45.

53. Bobrick, *East of the Sun*, 372–74.

54. Richard Hough, *The Fleet That Had to Die* (New York: Viking, 1958), 17, 120–43.

55. Bobrick, *East of the Sun*, 374.

56. Igor Gubert, letter to author, Sept. 8, 1991. The Russians founded new communities and cultural facilities. The Russian language was used exclusively in the schools as well as in the new Polytechnic Institute in Harbin. Even the Chinese residents who wanted an education learned Russian and attended Russian schools.

57. Emil Lengyel, *Siberia* (Garden City, N.Y.: Garden City Publishing Co., 1943), 135, 308. The 5,700-mile railroad was double-tracked in the 1930s.

58. Bobrick, *East of the Sun*, 393.

59. Betty M. Unterberger, *Intervention against Communism: Did the United States Try to Overthrow the Soviet Government, 1918–1920?* (College Station: Texas A&M University Lecture Series, 1986), 8, 10–11, 13, 22.

60. Bobrick, *East of the Sun*, 409–12. Wilson insisted that the Japanese forces also depart, but Japan did not withdraw them from Siberia until 1922 or from northern Sakhalin until 1925.

61. Lincoln, *Conquest of a Continent*, 300–301, 316. Sponsored by the Japanese, who provided gold and weapons, Semenov used armored trains on the Trans-Siberian Railroad for campaigns of terror and destruction.

62. Igor Gubert, letter to author, Sept. 8, 1991. Many of the refugees passed through Manchuria en route to Shanghai, Hong Kong, Australia, and even the United States. Semenov and others remained in the Russian colony in Manchuria. Col. Anatole Madievsky, the future father-in-law

of Igor Gubert, was one of them. They later united under Semenov's leadership and formed anti-Soviet paramilitary units.

63. Schwartz, *Tsars, Mandarins and Commissars*, 104–105, 116–18.

64. Igor Gubert, letter to author, Sept. 8, 1991. On the one hand, the refugees were irreconcilable White Russians. On the other, the loyal imported Soviet employees of the railroad were united with local Russian employees who chose to become Soviet citizens in order to retain their jobs.

65. Schwartz, *Tsars, Mandarins and Commissars*, 120–21. Having humiliated China in a short war (1894–95), Japan was aware of China's continuing helplessness and vulnerability. In 1931, the Japanese army seized strategic points in southern Manchuria as Japan made its first step in dominating the area.

66. Bobrick, *East of the Sun*, 412, 433–45. Millions of slave workers were condemned to serve in Siberian lumber, mine, factory, and farm projects and to build dams, power plants, and railroads.

67. Lincoln, *Conquest of a Continent*, 335, 352–54.

68. John H. Cloe, with Michael F. Monaghan, *Top Cover for America* (Anchorage, Alaska: Anchorage Chapter, Air Force Association; Missoula, Montana: Pictorial Histories Publishing, 1984), 2–3.

69. Ibid., 8–9. One of the planes, en route to the Far East, crashed near Port Moller on the Alaska Peninsula. The two-man crew, including Alva Harvey, survived. In 1942, Colonel Harvey surveyed the proposed ALSIB route from Alaska across Siberia.

70. Ibid., 5–7. In 1923 and again in 1926 and 1928, Eielson established himself as one of the true historic pioneers of Alaskan and arctic aviation. Among other early achievements, the team of Eielson and explorer George Hubert Wilkins sought to demonstrate whether an international arctic air route was practical.

71. Hunt, *Arctic Passage*, 290–95. In 1991, Soviet helicopter crews relocated the 1929 Eielson aircraft wreckage, salvaged it, and then delivered it to the Alaskaland Pioneer Air Museum in Fairbanks.

72. Anne Morrow Lindbergh, *North to the Orient* (New York: Harcourt Brace, 1935), 118–47. Lindberg arranged for fuel stockpiles at Karaginsk Island and Petropavlovsk.

73. Gerry Bruder, *Heroes of the Horizon* (Seattle: Alaska Northwest Books, 1991), 99–101.

74. Richard M. Ketchum, *Will Rogers, His Life and Times* (New York: American Heritage, 1973), 365–75. Will Rogers was no stranger to Siberia. In 1934, Will and Betty Rogers and two sons crossed Siberia by train and plane from Vladivostok to Moscow.

75. Von Hardesty, "Soviets Blaze Sky Trail over Top of World," *Air & Space* (Dec., 1987–Jan., 1988), 48–52.

76. Ibid., 53. Prior to his Moscow departure, Gromov lightened his plane by stripping it to the bare flying essentials.

77. Ibid., 54.

78. Otis Hays, Jr., *Home from Siberia:* The Secret Odysseys of Interned American Airmen in World War II (College Station: Texas A&M University Press, 1990), 60, 70–71, 106. The Russian Clipper evacuated American internees from Petropavlovsk to Khabarovsk in 1943–44. The flying boat was retired in late 1944 and reduced to scrap.

79. Cloe, *Top Cover for America*, 15–19. According to Arnold, a base was needed for emergency aircraft reception and supply as well as for cold-weather testing.

80. Edwin R. Carr, "History of the Northwest Air Route to Alaska, 1942–45," Record Group 018, File 306.01, U.S. Air Force Historical Research Center, Maxwell Air Force Base, Alabama, 1–7, 11–12 (hereafter cited as Carr, "History of Northwest Route"). Eventually, in 1939, the Civil Aviation Administration (CAA) sent Marshall Hoppin to Alaska and allocated funds for aeronautical aids as well as for improvement or construction of additional landing fields.

81. H. P. Willmott, *Empires in the Balance* (Annapolis: Naval Institute Press, 1982), 53–56. After Japan launched the Sino-Japanese war in 1937, Soviet-Japanese territorial disputes erupted on the Soviet border. In 1938–39, forces of Japan's Kwantung Army and the Red Army clashed in boundary skirmishes and two pitched battles.

82. Carr, "History of Northwest Route," 7–10.

83. Cloe, *Top Cover for America*, 22–23. Maj. Dale V. Gaffney helped to select the site. His name was linked with Ladd Field almost continuously throughout the war years.

84. Ronald H. Spector, *Eagle against the Sun* (New York: Free Press, 1985), 64.

85. John H. Cloe, *The Aleutian Warriors, Part I* (Anchorage, Alaska: Anchorage Chapter, Air Force Association; Missoula, Montana: Pictorial Histories Publishing, 1990), 6, 10, 15, 19–23. Although the completion of both Ladd and Elmendorf fields was not in sight, the first obsolete fighter and bombardment units of the future Eleventh Air Force arrived at Elmendorf Field in early 1941. Simultaneously, the vanguard of ground forces arrived to begin the garrisoning of Alaska. Buckner remained in his command position for four years and rose to become a lieutenant general. His Alaska Defense Force (ADF) was redesignated as the Alaska Defense Command (ADC) in 1941 and again as the independent Alaskan Department in 1943.

86. Ibid., 16–17. Later, as part of Dutch Harbor's protection, Buckner and Hoppin schemed to build secret bases at Cold Bay and Umnak Island.

CHAPTER 2

1. Jones, *Roads to Russia*, 6–7.
2. Ibid., 10–16.
3. Hubert P. van Tuyll, *Feeding the Bear: American Aid to the Soviet Union, 1941–1945* (New York: Greenwood Press, 1989), 3–4.
4. Spector, *Eagle against the Sun*, 68.
5. Van Tuyll, *Feeding the Bear*, 3.
6. Richard C. Lukas, *Eagles East: The Army Air Forces and the Soviet Union, 1941–1945* (Tallahassee: Florida State University Press, 1970), 15–16.
7. Cloe, *Aleutian Warriors*, 35–38.
8. Ibid., 37. Although twelve early warning radar sites were authorized, only two were in operation by June, 1942, one near Elmendorf Field and the other on Kodiak Island.
9. Ibid., 38.
10. Willmont, *Empires in the Balance*, 64.
11. Lukas, *Eagles East*, 18–24.
12. James A. Ryan, letter to author, Oct. 26, 1990.
13. *Nome Nugget*, Sept. 1, 1941.
14. James S. Russell, letter to author, Sept. 26, 1990. A decorated veteran of the Aleutian war (1942–43), Russell continued a career of high military achievement and became a four-star admiral before retirement.
15. Ray Wagner, *American Combat Planes* (Garden City, N.Y.: Doubleday, 1982), 309. In 1937, Soviet representatives bought three PBY flying boats at San Diego, California, and shipped them to the Soviet Union with a license to build additional flying boats there.
16. Associated Press release, Seattle, Sept. 4, 1941.
17. Lukas, *Eagles East*, 24.
18. Associated Press release, Seattle, Sept. 19, 1941.
19. Von Hardesty, *Red Phoenix: The Rise of Soviet Air Power, 1941–1945* (Washington: Smithsonian Institution Press, 1991), 245–46. Mikhail Gromov, whom Ambassador Oumansky called "the number one airman of the Soviet government," later became commander of the Red Air Force's 3rd Air Army (1942–43) and the 1st Air Army (1943–44).
20. Lukas, *Eagles East*, 24–27.

CHAPTER 3

1. Lukas, *Eagles East*, 95–102.
2. George C. Herring, Jr., *Aid to Russia, 1941–1946* (New York: Columbia University Press, 1973), 18.
3. W. Averill Harriman and Elie Abel, *Special Envoy to Churchill and Stalin, 1941–1946* (New York: Random House, 1975), 73–79.
4. Van Tuyll, *Feeding the Bear*, 5. Later, the Moscow Protocol was regarded as the First Protocol.
5. Ibid.
6. Jones, *Roads to Russia*, 68–69, 299–301. During the war, additional Second, Third, and Fourth Protocols were negotiated and approved in 1942, 1943, and 1944. In conjunction with the Fourth Protocol, a separate agreement provided Lend-Lease aid to the Red Army in the Far East for use when the Soviet Union went to war with Japan.
7. Herring, *Aid to Russia*, 42–43.
8. Van Tuyll, *Feeding the Bear*, 26.
9. Ibid., 27.
10. Ibid.; Jones, *Roads to Russia*, 112–13; John J. Stephan, *The Russian Far East: A History* (Stanford, Calif.: Stanford University Press, 1994), 238–39.
11. Van Tuyll, *Feeding the Bear*, 27.
12. John R. Deane, "Report of the Commanding General, United States Military Mission to Moscow, October 18, 1943–October 31, 1945," Record Group 334, National Archives, 71, 107.
13. Lukas, *Eagles East*, 19.
14. Ibid., 23.
15. Harriman and Abel, *Special Envoy*, 68.
16. Ilya Mazuruk, "Alaska-Siberia Airlift," *Soviet Life* (Oct., 1979), 30.
17. Robin Higham and Jacob W. Kipp, *Soviet Aviation and Air Power, a Historical View* (Boulder, Colo.: Westview Press, 1977), 172. Aeroflot, the Soviet Union's civil air fleet born in 1923 under the Red Air Force, became a separate organization after 1930. In World War II, Aeroflot was the military air transport arm of the Ministry of Defense.
18. Mazuruk, "Alaska-Siberia Airlift," 30.
19. Jones, *Roads to Russia*, 210–11.
20. Herring, *Aid to Russia*, 60–61.
21. Lukas, *Eagles East*, 97–101.
22. Ibid., 102.
23. Jones, *Roads to Russia*, 91.
24. Ibid., 300. Although the Second Protocol went into effect on July 1, it was not formally signed until Oct. 6.

25. Ibid., 93.
26. Lukas, *Eagles East*, 105.
27. Ibid., 106.
28. Mazuruk, "Alaska-Siberia Airlift," 30.
29. William H. Standley and Arthur A. Ageton, *Admiral Ambassador to Russia* (Washington: Regnery, 1955), 250.
30. Lukas, *Eagles East*, 125.
31. Herring, *Aid to Russia*, 67–69.
32. Lukas, *Eagles East*, 126–27.
33. Thomas J. Watson, Jr., and Peter Petre, *Father Son & Co.* (New York: Bantam, 1990), 100.
34. Westley J. Craven and James L. Cate, *The Army Air Forces in World War II*, vol. 7, chap. 6, "Northwest Air Route to Alaska" (Chicago: University of Chicago Press, 1958), 153–54.
35. Jones, *Roads to Russia*, 156.
36. Higham and Kipp, *Soviet Aviation*, 4. The C-47 was a military version of the Douglas DC-3 commercial passenger airliner. In 1936, the Soviet Union obtained a license from the Douglas Aircraft Company to produce the DC-3 as the Li-2. The C-47 became the military transport workhorse for the Army Air Force and was sought through Lend-Lease to supplement the Li-2 military transport fleet of the Red Air Force.
37. Lukas, *Eagles East*, 130.
38. Ibid., 130–31.
39. Jones, *Roads to Russia*, 158.
40. Lukas, *Eagles East*, 131.
41. Mazuruk, "Alaska-Siberia Airlift," 30.
42. Ibid.
43. Victor Perov, letter to author, June 15, 1992.
44. Ibid.
45. K. S. Coates and W. R. Morrison, *The Alaska Highway in World War II* (Norman: University of Oklahoma Press, 1992), 29–30.
46. Ibid., 31, 34.
47. Heath Twichell, *Northwest Epic: The Building of the Alaska Highway* (New York: St. Martin's Press, 1992), 55–56.
48. Ibid., 247–53.
49. Ibid., 53.
50. Ibid., 277–78.
51. Craven and Cate, "Northwest Air Route," 156.
52. Alaskan Division, Air Transport Command Historical Record Report, vol. 2, chap. 9, "Organization of the Northwest Ferrying Route," Record Group 018, File 306.01, U.S. Air Force Historical Research Center,

Maxwell Air Force Base, Alabama, 285–87 (hereafter cited as ATC Historical Report, "Organization of Northwest Route").

53.   Ibid., 299–304. Among ATC's early frustrations was the fact that responsibility for various facets of Northwest route operations was not centralized. At the start, too many commands had portions of the responsibility. Until solutions were later found, the intrusion of assorted military as well as diplomatic interests only complicated the route's serious logistical and organizational problems.

54.   Ibid., 322.

55.   Carr, "History of Northwest Route," 78.

56.   Ibid.

57.   ATC Historical Report, "Organization of Northwest Route," 317.

58.   Ibid., 322–25.

CHAPTER 4

1.   Carr, "History of Northwest Route," 177–80.

2.   Alaskan Division, Air Transport Command Historical Record Report, vol. 2, chap. 8, "Early Ferrying Activities on the Northwest Route," Record Group 018, File 306.01, U.S. Air Force Historical Research Center, Maxwell Air Force Base, Alabama, 269 (hereafter cited as ATC Historical Report, "Early Ferrying Activities").

3.   Ibid., 271.

4.   Ibid., 269–70.

5.   Elena Makarova, letter to author, Jan. 2, 1992.

6.   Lukas, *Eagles East*, 131.

7.   Elena Makarova, letter to author, Apr. 10, 1992.

8.   ATC Historical Report, "Early Ferrying Activities," 270.

9.   Ibid., 271–72.

10.   Ibid., 273.

11.   Hays, *Home from Siberia*, 40, 43. After the visit, Bradley recommended to the secretaries of war and state that they intervene diplomatically and request the Soviet authorities to parole the internees and put them to work.

12.   Lukas, *Eagles East*, 132–34.

13.   ATC Historical Report, "Early Ferrying Activities," 271.

14.   Ibid., 273–74. If the Soviets did not intend to use the ALSIB route, transports to service the route were no longer needed.

15.   Ibid., 278–80. Later, when the ALSIB route was irreversibly opened for massive ferrying operations, most of the responsibility for pilot transi-

tion training was gradually assumed by the Soviets themselves, using their own ALSIB route veterans.

16. Ibid., 274; Elena Makarova and Peter Gamov, letter to author, Jan. 2, 1992. According to Gamov's personal flight record, the flight was made on Oct. 7. Any confusion regarding the historic date probably was caused by crossing the international date line. The flight that began at Nome on Oct. 6 (Alaska time) landed at Markovo on Oct. 7. The reason for bypassing Uel'kal was not explained.

17. ATC Historical Report, "Early Ferrying Activities," 274–75.

18. Mazuruk, "Alaska-Siberia Airlift," 31.

19. David Sherl, "Alaska-Chukotka-Front: The Airlift That Never Failed," *Soviet Life* (Dec., 1986), 20.

20. Craven and Cate, "Northwest Air Route," 159.

21. Colonel Hart's last official function was greeting Wendell Willkie, whose 1942 world tour was in the interest of his *One World* concept. Willkie's flight route was completed over a part of the ALSIB route to Alaska. He overnighted at Ladd Field on Oct. 10–11.

22. ATC Historical Report, "Organization of Northwest Route," 326–30.

23. Ibid., 333–34.

24. Carr, "History of Northwest Route," 79.

25. Ibid.

26. Craven and Cate, "Northwest Air Route," 158. However, the wing commander later gained operational control of the ferrying pilots while they were in the wing's operational area.

27. Ibid., 155.

28. ATC Historical Report, "Early Ferrying Activities," 258.

29. Carr, "History of Northwest Route," 179.

30. Ibid., 190.

31. Watson and Petre, *Father Son & Co.*, 105–109.

32. As noted in miscellaneous 1942–43 Alaska Defense Command G-2 reports and reconfirmed in G-2 Report no. 98, annex 7, Apr. 8, 1944.

33. George Kisevalter, letters to author, Feb. 20, Mar. 24, and Apr. 6, 1992; Elena Makarova, letter to author, Feb. 11, 1993.

34. Carr, "History of Northwest Route," 178.

35. Craven and Cate, "Northwest Air Route," 168.

36. Jones, *Roads to Russia*, 277 (table 2).

37. Carr, "History of Northwest Route," 190.

38. Ibid., 85–86.

39. Ibid., 87–88.

40. Ibid., 89–90.

41. Ibid., 90–91. In addition, three new auxiliary airfields in Alaska were established. One was a satellite field at Mile 26 east of Fairbanks for Ladd Field's excess aircraft. Another was a satellite field near Nome to care for the transient Lend-Lease overflow. The third was at Moses Point, an emergency field on the ALSIB route between Galena and Nome.
42. Ibid., 93–95.
43. Twichell, *Northwest Epic,* 279.

CHAPTER 5

1. Several were born in Russia during World War I but their parents carried the infants into exile.
2. Igor Gubert, letter to author, Aug. 15, 1991.
3. Van Tuyll, *Feeding the Bear,* 11.
4. G-2 Report no. 181, annex 7, Nov. 10, 1945. Responsibility for maintaining entry and departure records was transferred to the Department of Justice's Immigration and Naturalization Service after the war's end.
5. Letter report from Michael Gavrisheff to George Kisevalter, commander of the Alaska Defense Command's I&I Russian section, Oct. 12, 1943.
6. Michael Gavrisheff, letter to author, Jan. 16, 1990; George Kisevalter, letter to author, Jan. 17, 1990.
7. David Chavchavadze, *Crowns and Trenchcoats: A Russian Prince in the CIA* (New York: Atlantic International Publications, 1990), 111.
8. Igor Gubert, letter to author, July 16, 1990.
9. Chavchavadze, *Crowns and Trenchcoats,* 110, 111, 116.
10. Michael Gavrisheff, letters to author, Jan. 16 and Aug. 20, 1990; Igor Gubert, letter to author, July 16, 1990.
11. Igor Gubert, letter to author, July 16, 1990.
12. George Kisevalter, letters to author, Aug. 6 and Sept. 10, 1990, and Aug. 2, 1992.
13. Michael Gavrisheff, letters to author, Jan. 10, Aug. 20, and Sept. 1, 1990.
14. Igor Gubert, letters to author, Aug. 15, Sept. 8, and Dec. 12, 1991, and July 25, 1992.
15. Gubert recalled that the Japanese intelligence service recruited young White Russians and sent them across the Soviet border, only to have them fall into the hands of the Soviet NKVD and be executed. The Japanese also used units of the White Russian paramilitary organization to occupy White Russian settlements in the forward border area. Colonel Madievsky was in charge of one settlement.
16. Chavchavadze, *Crowns and Trenchcoats,* 12–109.
17. David Chavchavadze, letters to author, Aug. 2, and 10, 1990.

18. Igor Gubert, letters to author, July 16 and Aug. 16, 1990; Michael Gav-
    risheff, letters to author, Jan. 16, Sept. 1, and 20, 1990; George Kiseval-
    ter, letters to author, Jan. 17 and Aug. 6, 1990.

CHAPTER 6

1. Van Tuyll, *Feeding the Bear*, 42–43.
2. Michael Gavrisheff, letter to author, Feb. 12, 1990.
3. G-2 Russian Report, Apr. 24, 1943.
4. Michael Gavrisheff, letter to author, Feb. 12, 1990; G-2 Russian Report,
   Mar. 27, 1943. However, later in 1943 when Soviet restrictions appeared
   to relax and family members were permitted to join senior officials in
   Alaska, the officers and their wives were persuaded to have quiet din-
   ners with Americans.
5. I&I Russian section commander, letter to all liaison interpreters, Aug.
   11, 1943.
6. George Kisevalter, letter to author, Aug. 6, 1990.
7. G-2 Russian Report, May 1, 1943.
8. G-2 Report no. 73, annex 7, Oct. 16, 1943.
9. G-2 Reports no. 53, annex 8, May 29, 1943; no. 66, annex 4, Aug. 28,
   1943; and no. 70, annex 7, Sept. 25, 1943.
10. Associated Press release, New York, May 20, 1943.
11. In 1944, the Soviets were more relaxed and Japan was no longer a taboo
    subject. After the Soviet Union denounced its neutrality pact with Japan
    in early 1945, the Soviets were eager to condemn Japan.
12. G-2 Reports no. 61, annex 4, July 24, 1943, and no. 63, annex 4, Aug. 7,
    1943.
13. G-2 Russian Report, Mar. 27, 1943; G-2 Report no. 58, annex 8, July 3,
    1943.
14. Blake W. Smith (Canadian Northwest route historian), letter to author,
    Jan. 2, 1990.
15. Michael Gavrisheff, undated letter to George Kisevalter, summer,
    1943.
16. Ibid. Gavrisheff later recommended that some of the I&I liaison inter-
    preters be transferred from Fairbanks to Nome because of a greater need
    there.
17. Igor Gubert, letter to author, July 25, 1992.
18. Ibid.
19. ATC Historical Report, "Early Ferrying Activities," 279.
20. Craven and Cate, "Northwest Air Route," 166.
21. Extract of address, "Aviation Lend-Lease, Alaska to Russia," by Fyodor

D. Alberti, Moscow Institute of Civil Aviation Engineers, at the ALSIB Lend-Lease Reunion, Fairbanks, Alaska, July 10, 1992.

22. Ibid.

23. Records of the administrator, Fort Richardson National Cemetery, Alaska. All thirteen were listed as crash victims in 1943.

24. Craven and Cate, "Northwest Air Route," 165.

25. Carr, "History of Northwest Route," 190. Total Second Protocol deliveries to Ladd Field numbered 1,107. Protocol commitments called for 1,420 (although the original goal had been 1,704), leaving a shortfall of 313 to be carried over for future delivery.

26. G-2 Report no. 60, annex 8, July 17, 1943.

27. Oleg Chechin, "Rescue of a Soviet Navigator," *Soviet Life* (Nov., 1989), 39–42.

28. Paul Solka, "Rescuing a Russian from the Wilderness," *Fairbanks (Alaska) Daily News-Miner*, Mar. 10, 1989.

29. The two versions of the Demyanenko rescue as reported by Chechin and Solka contained a variation in fact. One stated that the period covered by the search for the missing airman was a matter of weeks, the other a matter of days.

30. Chechin, "Rescue of a Soviet Navigator," 42; *Fairbanks (Alaska) Daily News-Miner*, Aug. 31, 1944.

31. John R. Deane, *The Strange Alliance* (New York: Viking, 1947), 233–34.

32. G-2 Russian Reports, Apr. 19 and 24, 1943.

33. Alaska Defense Command CI-R1 Summary Military Intelligence Report, "Pvt. John Oliver White, ASN 39950081, 83rd Depot Supply Squadron, Ladd Field, Alaska, 14 August 1943," Record Group 338, National Archives.

34. Ibid.

35. Edward J. Fortier, "The Death of Pvt. John White," *Fairbanks (Alaska) Daily News-Miner*, July 17 and 24, 1988. Some Fairbanks residents still believe that John White's death was not an accident.

36. Craven and Cate, "Northwest Air Route," 165.

37. G-2 Report no. 68, annex 7, Sept. 11, 1943.

38. Elena Makarova and Peter Gamov, letter to author, Jan. 2, 1992.

CHAPTER 7

1. Extract of address, "The Role of Lend-Lease in Russia's Struggle against Fascism," by Georgi A. Kimanyou, Russian Academy of Sciences, at the ALSIB Lend-Lease Reunion, Fairbanks, Alaska, July 10, 1992.

2. Hardesty, *Red Phoenix*, 220.

3. Ibid.
4. Jones, *Roads to Russia*, 277.
5. Ibid., 278.
6. G-2 Report no. 80, annex 7, Dec. 4, 1943.
7. G-2 Report no. 86, annex 7, Jan. 15, 1944.
8. Hardesty, *Red Phoenix*, 141.
9. G-2 Report no. 71, annex 7, Oct. 2, 1943. American women pilots were not engaged in Lend-Lease ferrying operations in Canada and Alaska.
10. G-2 Report no. 86, annex 7, Jan. 15, 1944.
11. G-2 Reports no. 67, annex 7, Sept. 4, 1943 and no. 69, annex 7, Sept. 18, 1943.
12. George Kisevalter, letter to author, Sept. 18, 1989.
13. G-2 Reports no. 52, annex 8, May 22, 1943; no. 56, annex 8, June 19, 1943; and no. 81, annex 7, Dec. 11, 1943.
14. G-2 Report no. 73, annex 7, Oct. 16, 1943.
15. G-2 Report no. 90, annex 7, Feb. 11, 1944.
16. Interview with Elwood Nash in *Alaska History News* (Fall, 1991). Nash was one of the contract mechanics.
17. Hays, *Home from Siberia*, 203. The fuel of choice was wood.
18. G-2 Reports no. 81, annex 7, Dec. 11, 1943 and no. 102, annex 7, May 6, 1944.
19. G-2 Report no. 62, annex 7, July 31, 1943.
20. G-2 Report no. 64, annex 7, Aug. 14, 1943.
21. G-2 Report no. 65, annex 7, Aug. 21, 1943.
22. G-2 Reports no. 62, annex 7, July 31, 1943, and no. 65, annex 7, Aug. 21, 1943.
23. G-2 Report no. 88, annex 7, Jan. 29, 1944.
24. G-2 Report no. 64, annex 7, Aug. 14, 1943.
25. G-2 Report no. 70, annex 7, Sept. 25, 1943.
26. G-2 Report no. 88, annex 7, Jan. 29, 1944.
27. G-2 Report no. 63, annex 7, Aug. 7, 1943.
28. G-2 Report no. 88, annex 7, Aug. 28, 1943.
29. G-2 Report no. 67, annex 7, Sept. 4, 1943.
30. Igor Gubert, letter to author, July 26, 1992.
31. Igor Gubert letter to author, June 26, 1992.
32. Igor Gubert letter to author, July 25, 1992.
33. Ibid.
34. G-2 Reports no. 64, annex 7, Aug. 14, 1943; no. 65, annex 7, Aug. 21, 1943; no. 67, annex 7, Sept. 4, 1943; and no. 80, annex 7, Dec. 4, 1943.
35. G-2 Report no. 71, annex 7, Oct. 2, 1943.
36. Ibid.

37. G-2 Report no. 73, annex 7, Oct. 16, 1943.
38. Otis Hays, Jr., "The Silent Years in Alaska," *Alaska Journal* (1986 anthology), 140–47.
39. Drew Pearson, "Washington Merry-Go-Round," Sept. 16, 1943, Lyndon Baines Johnson Library archives, Austin, Texas.
40. G-2 Report no. 73, annex 4, Oct. 16, 1943.
41. Chavchavadze, *Crowns and Trenchcoats*, 114.
42. G-2 Report no. 73, annex 7, Oct. 16, 1943.
43. Ibid.
44. Ibid.
45. G-2 Report no. 76, annex 7, Nov. 6, 1943; Elena Makarova, letter to author, Oct. 4, 1992. Makarova recalled having ordered a coffin for the little girl, whose body was buried in a Fairbanks cemetery.
46. G-2 Report no. 76, annex 7, Nov. 6, 1943.
47. George Kisevalter, letter to author, Feb. 25, 1990.
48. G-2 Report no. 76, annex 7, Nov. 6, 1943.

CHAPTER 8
1. G-2 Report no. 80, annex 7, Dec. 4, 1943.
2. Ibid.
3. G-2 Report no. 79, annex 4, Nov. 27, 1943; Washington, D.C., Associated Press release, Nov. 24, 1943.
4. G-2 Report no. 80, annex 4, Dec. 4, 1943.
5. George Kisevalter, letter to author, Dec. 5, 1990.
6. Chavchavadze, *Crowns and Trenchcoats*, 110.
7. Ibid.
8. Ibid., 111.
9. Ibid.
10. Ibid., 112.
11. George Kisevalter, letter to author, Feb. 6, 1993.
12. G-2 Report no. 81, annex 7, Dec. 11, 1943.
13. G-2 Report no. 84, annex 7, Jan. 1, 1944.
14. G-2 Report no. 86, annex 7, Jan. 15, 1944.
15. Brian Garfield, *The Thousand-Mile War* (New York: Doubleday, 1969), 292.
16. Hays, *Home from Siberia*, 66–67.
17. G-2 Report no. 84, annex 7, Jan. 1, 1944.
18. Ibid.
19. G-2 Report no. 79, annex 7, Nov. 27, 1943. Six months later, in June, 1944, the search for housing, either single or multiple dwellings, continued without success.

20. G-2 Report no. 80, annex 7, Dec. 4, 1943.
21. Carr, "History of Northwest Route," 193.
22. Ibid., 194.
23. G-2 Report no. 94, annex 7, Mar. 11, 1944.
24. G-2 Report no. 91, annex 7, Feb. 19, 1944.
25. G-2 Report no. 92, annex 7, Feb. 26, 1944.
26. G-2 Report no. 83, annex 7, Dec. 25, 1943.
27. G-2 Report no. 97, annex 7, Apr. 1, 1944.
28. G-2 Report no. 96, annex 7, Mar. 25, 1944.
29. G-2 Report no. 102, annex 7, May 6, 1944.
30. G-2 Report no. 106, annex 7, June 3, 1944.
31. Associated Press release, Washington, D.C., May 20, 1944.
32. *Fairbanks (Alaska) Daily News-Miner*, May 23, 1944.
33. Hays, *Home from Siberia*, 97. Wallace was not aware that an internment camp near Tashkent was waiting to receive another group of American airmen whose bombers had crashed in Siberia.
34. *Fairbanks (Alaska) Daily News-Miner*, July 4, 1944.
35. Craven and Cate, "Northwest Air Route," 164.
36. G-2 Report no. 110, annex 7, July 1, 1944.
37. G-2 Reports no. 104, annex 7, May 20, 1944, and no. 106, annex 7, June 3, 1944.
38. Elena Makarova, letter to author, Jan. 2, 1992.
39. G-2 Report no. 110, annex 7, July 1, 1944.
40. Elena Makarova, interview at the ALSIB Lend-Lease Reunion, Fairbanks, Alaska, July 9, 1992.
41. Chavchavadze, *Crowns and Trenchcoats*, 112.
42. Carr, "History of Northwest Route," 197.
43. G-2 Report no. 106, annex 7, June 3, 1944.
44. Alaskan Division, Air Transport Command Historical Record Report, vol. 2, "June 1944 Operations," Record Group 018, File 306.01, U.S. Air Force Historical Research Center, Maxwell Air Force Base, Alabama, 3–5 (hereafter cited as ATC Historical Report, "[Month] 1944 Operations").
45. Craven and Cate, "Northwest Air Route," 165.

CHAPTER 9

1. Jones, *Roads to Russia*, 171.
2. Harriman and Abel, *Special Envoy*, 343.
3. Stalin refused to meet in Basra, Iraq, as Roosevelt proposed.
4. Jones, *Roads to Russia*, 174.
5. Carr, "History of Northwest Route," 198. The only exceptions were

fifty P-39 fighters that were flown from North Africa to the Persian Gulf in order to complete a delivery already in progress at the end of the Third Protocol period.

6. ATC Historical Report, "July 1944 Operations," 1.
7. Carr, "History of Northwest Route," 199.
8. Ibid., 200–201.
9. Ibid., 199.
10. ATC Historical Report, "September–October 1944 Operations," 3.
11. Craven and Cate, "Northwest Air Route," 166–67.
12. Igor Gubert, letter to author, Dec. 4, 1992.
13. Ibid.
14. Michael Gavrisheff, letter to author, Feb. 12, 1990.
15. Ibid.
16. Michael Gavrisheff, letter to author, July 3, 1944. At that time (1944), the author was General Buckner's staff supervisor of Soviet-American liaison activities.
17. Chavchavadze, *Crowns and Trenchcoats*, 113.
18. Ibid., 116–19.
19. Harriman and Abel, *Special Envoy*, 408–409.
20. Chavchavadze, *Crowns and Trenchcoats*, 114.
21. Michael Gavrisheff, letter to author, Jan. 6, 1990.
22. Harriman and Abel, *Special Envoy*, 152–53.
23. Deane, *Strange Alliance*, 246–49.
24. Herring, *Aid to Russia*, 183.
25. Harriman and Abel, *Special Envoy*, 364, 400.
26. Ibid., 408–409.
27. Lukas, *Eagles East*, 178n.
28. Alaskan Department Historical Report (undated draft), "Lend Lease Ferry Program," Record Group 338, National Archives.
29. Hardesty, *Red Phoenix*, 247–48.
30. Deane, *Strange Alliance*, 255–66.
31. Harriman and Abel, *Special Envoy*, 441.
32. Chavchavadze, *Crowns and Trenchcoats*, 121.
33. Igor Gubert, letter to author, Nov. 1, 1992.
34. Ibid.
35. Harriman and Abel, *Special Envoy*, 441–43.
36. Igor Gubert, letter to author, Nov. 1, 1992.
37. Ibid., Dec. 4, 1992.
38. Ibid., Nov. 1, 1992.

CHAPTER 10

1. Deane, *Strange Alliance*, 254; Stan Cohen, *The Forgotten War*, vol. 1 (Missoula, Montana: Pictorial Histories Publishing, 1981), 53.

2. Everett A. Long and Ivan Y. Neganblya, *Cobras over the Tundra* (Fairbanks, Alaska: Arktika Publishing, 1992), 42, 43.

3. Jones, *Roads to Russia*, 210, 231.

4. Admiral Russell, letter to author, Sept. 26, 1990; delayed Associated Press release, Cold Bay, Alaska, Aug. 8, 1945; Cohen, *Forgotten War*, vol. 3, 44–47.

5. Herring, *Aid to Russia*, 206.

6. Carr, "History of Northwest Route," 203.

7. Long and Neganblya, *Cobras over the Tundra*, 103. In February, 1945, the 1st Ferrying Aviation Division was named a Red Banner unit in ceremonies conducted at the Yakutsk air base.

8. Carr, "History of Northwest Route," 199.

9. Unpublished Alaskan Department G-2 summary, "Notes on Valeri Tihonovich Minakov and His Escape from the USSR," in author's files. The draft paper was prepared after G-2 Special Agent Charles Dowling, accompanied by Special Agent Freely and I&I Sergeant Farafontoff, went to St. Lawrence Island in early August, 1945.

10. Ibid. Minakov's kayak, hidden from view in a shed at Gambell, was burned to destroy any evidence of Minakov's presence on the island.

11. G-2 Report no. 95, annex 7, Mar. 18, 1944. As early as 1943, trained Siberian Eskimos became part of the Soviet intelligence apparatus in the Bering Strait area. They were used for coastal and technical intelligence on American ship movements, cargoes, armaments, and related data.

12. Harriman and Abel, *Special Envoy*, 490–91.

13. Igor Gubert, letter to author, Sept. 8, 1991.

14. Schwartz, *Tsars, Mandarins and Commissars*, 143–44.

15. Stephan, *The Kurils*, 162–66.

16. Carr, "History of Northwest Route," 204.

17. Although some sources have insisted that the total aircraft count was 7,925, they included the B-24 bomber that General Bradley abandoned at Yakutsk in November, 1942, while en route to, not from, Alaska.

18. Elena Makarova and Aleksandr Kotgarov, letters to author, June 15, 1992; Hays, *Home from Siberia*, 213. Of the thirty-seven U.S. bombers that crashed in Siberia, the Soviets salvaged at least nine. According to the Ministry of Defense archives in Moscow, seven of them were from the Aleutians. One army B-24 bomber was allocated to the Red Air Force in the Far East. Two other army B-25s and four navy PV-1s were

assigned to a Petropavlovsk-based regiment of the 128th Mixed Aviation Division and used for border patrolling and training.

19. Sherl, "Alaska-Chukotka-Front, the Airlift That Never Failed," 50.

20. Elena Makarova, letter to author, Jan. 2, 1992. On Apr. 25, 1945, Senior Sgt. Nicholas P. Tiurin married Lt. Natasha Fenelonova, a staff technical interpreter. Their wedding had the approval of General Obrazkov, who registered the marriage at the Soviet embassy in Washington. Fenelonova also served as a personal interpreter for General Obrazkov's wife at Fairbanks.

21. Chavchavadze, *Crowns and Trenchcoats*, 129.

22. Ibid., 130.

23. Ibid. De Moore apparently was suspicious of Chavchavadze's eagerness to accompany the Soviet navy group. Chavchavadze recalled that when he said good-bye, de Moore displayed his pistol and said, "David, if you don't come back, sooner or later I'll shoot you!" In 1947, the two encountered each other in New York City. De Moore made no mention of his threat and neither did Chavchavadze.

24. Igor Gubert, letter to author, Dec. 4, 1992.

25. Cohen, *Forgotten War*, vol. 3, 101.

26. Cohen, *Forgotten War*, vol. 1, 235.

POSTSCRIPT

1. Information regarding the post-World War II lives of former U.S. liaison officers George Kisevalter, Michael Gavrisheff, Igor Gubert, and David Chavchavadze, as well as former Soviet technical interpreters Elena Makarova and Natasha Fenelonova and Soviet ALSIB aviation veterans Peter Gamov and Nicholas Tiurin was compiled from frequent correspondence during the years 1990–93.

2. Igor Gubert, letter to author, Jan. 20, 1993.

3. Frank J. Daugherty, "Escape from Siberia," *Alaska* (July, 1971), 52.

4. Jones, *Roads to Russia*, 293.

5. George R. Jordan, *From Major Jordan's Diaries* (New York: Harcourt Brace, 1952).

6. Jones, *Roads to Russia*, 295.

7. Silvio Sclocchini, letter to author, July, 1989.

8. Maj. Gen. Ilya Mazuruk, Lt. Gen. Michael Machin, Maj. Gen. Mark Shevelev, Capt. Peter Gamov, Maj. Fyodor Zheviakov, Capt. Victor Perov, Capt. Dmitri Ostrovenko, and Capt. David Sherl, "Let's Meet Again!" *Soviet Life* (April, 1988), 57–59.

9. Victor Perov, letter to author, June 15, 1992.

10. V. D. Len'kov, G. L. Silant'ev and A. K. Staniukovich, *The Koman-*

dorskii Camp of the Bering Expedition (Anchorage: Alaska Historical Society, 1992), 148–50.

11. Moscow, Associated Press release, Dec. 14, 1993.

12. Anchorage, Alaska, Associated Press release, Feb. 27, 1993.

13. Igor Krekshin, "TransSiberian Railway, Yesterday, Today, Tomorrow," *Russian Life* and RIA *Novosti Moscow* (Summer, 1994), 22–31.

Appendix A
Aircraft Deliveries via ALSIB

Type of Aircraft	Delivered at Factory	Lost in U.S.	Lost via NW route	Accepted at Ladd Field
Transports				
C-46	1	0	0	1
C-47	709	2	0	707
Fighters				
P-39	2,689	37	34	2,618
P-40	50	0	2	48
P-47	3	0	0	3
P-63	2,418	10	11	2,397
Light Bombers				
A-20	1,396	24	9	1,363
Medium Bombers				
B-25	737	1	3	733
Trainers				
AT6-F	54	0	0	54
Totals	8,057	74	59	7,924

Appendix B
Soviet Personnel in Alaska

By December, 1943, the Soviet presence, both civilian and military, had been firmly established by the Soviet Purchasing Commission and the Soviet Military Mission. The permanent Soviets numbered approximately 160, although that number fluctuated with unscheduled arrivals and departures.

SOVIET PURCHASING COMMISSION

Anisimov, Alexis A.	Chief of Commission
Anisimova, Dina V. (Mrs.)	Secretary
Byrd, Bess (U.S. citizen)	Typist
Jurist, S. N. (U.S. citizen)	Translator
Kharitonov, Michael E.	Auditor and treasurer
Mazur, Evgeniya F. (Mrs.)	Typist
Mazur, Anatoly A.	Office boy, age 15
Sosedov, Michael V.	Senior Technical Lieutenant

LADD FIELD DEPENDENTS

Kalinnikova, Nina S. (Mrs.)	Wife of Major Kalinnikov
Kalinnikov, Vladimir	Son, age 6
Kiseleva, Maria P. (Mrs.)	Wife of Colonel Kiselev; secretary to Soviet Military Mission
Machina, Lydia A. (Mrs.)	Wife of Colonel Machin
Machin, Alexander	Son, age 4
Machin, Gennady	Son, age 8

Strizhkova, Valentina (Mrs.)	Wife of Lieutenant Colonel Strizhkov
Strizhkov, Roman	Son, age 4
Yatzkevich, Elena D. (Mrs.)	Wife of Major Yatzkevich
Yatzkevich, Anatoly	Son, age 7

NOME DEPENDENTS

Gubina, Galena I. (Mrs.)	Wife of Captain Gubin
Gubin, Alexander	Son, age 4
Gubin, George	Son, age 6

LADD FIELD PERMANENT GARRISON

Machin, Michael G.	Colonel, Soviet Military Mission commander
Kiselev, Peter S.	Colonel, engineer, and executive
Strizhkov, Andrew I.	Lieutenant Colonel, engineer
Borovikov, Narkiss P.	Major, engineer
Chernikov, Jacob I.	Major, engineer
Kalinnikov, Nicholas N.	Major, engineer
Radominov, Eugene G.	Major, engineer
Yatzkevich, Alexander P.	Major, engineer
Berezko, Semyon	Captain, engineer
Chernevksy, Vadim P.	Captain, engineer
Pokrovsky, Roman P.	Captain, engineer
Vologov, Dimitri M.	Captain, intelligence
Constantinov, Andrew A.	Senior Technical Lieutenant
Smirnov, Gregory T.	Senior Technical Lieutenant
Vorontniuk, Alexander H.	Senior Technical Lieutenant
Zoubry, Yefin I.	Senior Technical Lieutenant
Komar, Makary F.	Lieutenant, cryptographer
Aristarkhov, Peter T.	Technical Lieutenant
Dudko, Ivan F.	Technical Lieutenant
Golev, Constantine P.	Technical Lieutenant
Nikulin, Vassily A.	Technical Lieutenant
Pankov, Vassily A.	Technical Lieutenant
Shevchenko, N. S.	Technical Lieutenant
Shevchuk, Victor A.	Technical Lieutenant
Slobodskoy, Naum I.	Technical Lieutenant
Tkal, L. M.	Technical Lieutenant
Smirnov, Eugene I.	Junior Lieutenant
Doubovitsky, Vladimir G.	Junior Technical Lieutenant

Ozhogov, Peter I.	Junior Technical Lieutenant
Gnedounets, Nicholas E.	Warrant Officer
Kanishchev, N. V.	Master Sergeant
Kostin, Jacob P.	Master Sergeant
Prozora, Yevdokim R.	Master Sergeant
Mousienko, Vassily J.	Senior Sergeant
Shibayev, Ivan P.	Senior Sergeant
Shramkov, Ivan A.	Senior Sergeant
Tiurin, Nicholas P.	Senior Sergeant
Karnaoukh, Nicholas Z.	Sergeant
Fenelonova, Natasha	Lieutenant, technical interpreter
Makarova, Elena A.	Lieutenant, technical interpreter

NOME PERMANENT GARRISON

Grigorenko, Nicholas M.	Captain, garrison commander
Gubin, Michael M.	Captain, intelligence, and engineer
Lysogorsky, Alexander S.	Captain, communications
Burechek, Serge I.	Senior Lieutenant, communications
Luzhanski, Grigory	Senior Lieutenant, mechanic
Kudriavtsev, Michael	Lieutenant, mechanic
Yashkin, Vladimir	Lieutenant, mechanic
Fedorenko, Nicholas	Senior Sergeant, mechanic
Kortenko, Peter N.	Senior Sergeant, mechanic
Druzhininsky, Vassily G.	Sergeant, radio technician
Volynets, Vladimir D.	Sergeant, radio technician

1ST FERRYING AVIATION REGIMENT
HEADQUARTERS

Vasin, Nikifor S.	Lieutenant Colonel, commander
Kobin, Michael D.	Major, regimental navigator
Zeiklin, Boris M.	Major, chief of staff
Lomov, Fedor S.	Captain, assistant chief of staff
Zotov, Peter G.	Captain, assistant commander
Kiyan, Jacob S.	Technical Lieutenant, engineer
Dochar, Paul S.	Junior Lieutenant, radio operations
Kouzmin, Alexander F.	Junior Lieutenant, radio operations

FIGHTER SQUADRONS

Zhevlakov, Fedor A.	Major, squadron commander
Ereminsky, Alexander A.	Captain, assistant squadron commander

Gorchakov, Eugene I.	Captain, squadron commander
Novikov, Anatoly G.	Captain, squadron commander
Rezvov, Constantine A.	Captain, flight leader
Senchenko, Nicholas M.	Captain, assistant squadron commander
Babakhin, Ivan E.	Senior Lieutenant, pilot
Biblioshvili, Nicholas N.	Senior Lieutenant, flight leader
Bojrmistrov, Ivan I.	Senior Lieutenant, assistant squadron commander
Diuzhikov, A. I.	Senior Lieutenant, pilot
Shchegolev, Leo D.	Senior Lieutenant, pilot
Shishkin, Nicholas P.	Senior Lieutenant, pilot
Souvorov, Vladimir I.	Senior Lieutenant, flight leader
Vaskov, Michael J.	Senior Lieutenant, flight leader
Vorobiov, I. A.	Senior Lieutenant, flight leader
Yagodkin, Paul S.	Senior Lieutenant, pilot
Batyshev, Alexander J.	Lieutenant, pilot
Grigoriev, Ivan N.	Lieutenant, pilot
Kirin, Sergei D.	Lieutenant, pilot
Kocherov, Gavrila T.	Lieutenant, flight leader
Romanov, S. S.	Lieutenant, pilot
Bespalov, Leonid P.	Junior Lieutenant, pilot
Degtyarev, Constantine N.	Junior Lieutenant, pilot
Makarov, A. P.	Junior Lieutenant, pilot

BOMBER SQUADRONS

Ivanov, Constantine V.	Captain, flight leader
Barchenko, Constantine P.	Captain, squadron commander
Lebedev, C. M.	Captain, flight leader
Antokhin, Fedor V.	Senior Lieutenant, flight leader
Bocharev, Constantine P.	Senior Lieutenant, assistant squadron commander
Demyanenko, Constantine P.	Senior Lieutenant, squadron navigator
Gamov, Peter P.	Senior Lieutenant, squadron commander
Komar, Mark I.	Senior Lieutenant, assistant flight leader
Melyayev, Alexander I.	Senior Lieutenant, flight navigator
Novikov, Peter I.	Senior Lieutenant, pilot

Platkov, George F.	Senior Lieutenant, flight leader
Sverchkov, Vassily L.	Senior Lieutenant, squadron navigator
Titov, Michael N.	Senior Lieutenant, pilot
Vorobiov, P. J.	Senior Lieutenant, pilot
Krisanov, Alexis P.	Senior Technical Lieutenant, flight engineer
Agourenko, Alexis M.	Lieutenant, pilot
Bochkanov, V. I.	Lieutenant, pilot
Dmitriev, Nicholas G.	Lieutenant, flight engineer
Fedorov, Alexander D.	Lieutenant, pilot
Gorbenko, J. D.	Lieutenant, flight leader
Sorokin, Alexander S.	Lieutenant, flight navigator
Trapeznikov, Fedor I.	Lieutenant, flight leader
Trepolsky, Vladimir V.	Lieutenant, flight navigator
Vorona, Michael A.	Lieutenant, pilot
Karpov, Gregory L.	Technical Lieutenant, flight engineer
Ivashkevich, Nicholas A.	Technical Lieutenant, flight engineer
Susin, N. L.	Technical Lieutenant, flight engineer
Talalaikin, Vassily I.	Technical Lieutenant, flight engineer
Zvorono, C. K.	Junior Lieutenant, flight radio operator
Panchev, George A.	Master Sergeant, flight radio operator
Dedkov, A. D.	Senior Sergeant, flight radio operator
Gordienko, Peter F.	Senior Sergeant, flight radio operator
Kouznetsov, Alexander E.	Senior Sergeant, flight radio operator
Loukin, Michael A.	Senior Sergeant, flight radio operator
Manilov, I. P.	Senior Sergeant, flight radio operator
Sirnev, Eugene I.	Senior Sergeant, flight radio operator
Grebennikov, Nicholas J.	Sergeant, flight radio operator

Khomiakov, Andrew O.	Sergeant, flight radio operator
Nosakin, Ivan I.	Sergeant, flight radio operator
Pelageychenko, Peter A.	Sergeant, flight radio operator
Tzisar, V. P.	Sergeant, flight radio operator
Zuey, Ivan M.	Sergeant, flight radio operator

TRANSPORT CREWS

Finogenov, V. V.	Captain, squadron commander
Khasayev, Roman A.	Captain, ship commander
Khlaptsev, V. I.	Captain, ship commander
Dzugutov, Muktar M.	Senior Lieutenant, ship commander
Voukov, V. P.	Senior Lieutenant
Moushtakov, George I.	Lieutenant, flight radio operator
Popanov, Paul R.	Lieutenant, copilot
Ustinov, Alexis D.	Lieutenant
Belov, Maxim E.	Technical Lieutenant, flight engineer
Dopkin, Sergei M.	Technical Lieutenant, flight engineer
Pismarev, Victor A.	Technical Lieutenant, flight engineer
Danilov, P. O.	Junior Lieutenant, copilot
Gordeyev, Ivan I.	Junior Lieutenant, flight radio operator
Kirenko, N. A.	Junior Lieutenant

Bibliography

BOOKS

Bobrick, Benson. *East of the Sun*. New York: Poseidon Press, 1992.

Bruder, Gerry. *Heroes of the Horizon*. Seattle: Alaska Northwest Books, 1991.

Chavchavadze, David. *Crowns and Trenchcoats: A Russian Prince in the CIA*. New York: Atlantic International Publications, 1990.

Chevigny, Hector. *Russian America: The Great Alaskan Venture, 1741–1867*. New York: Viking, 1965.

Cloe, John H. *The Aleutian Warriors*. Pt. 1. Anchorage, Alaska: Anchorage Chapter, Air Force Association; Missoula, Montana: Pictorial Histories Publishing, 1990.

———, with Michael F. Monaghan. *Top Cover for America*. Anchorage, Alaska: Anchorage Chapter, Air Force Association; Missoula, Montana: Pictorial Histories Publishing, 1984.

Coates, K. S., and W. R. Morrison. *The Alaska Highway in World War II*. Norman: University of Oklahoma Press, 1992.

Cohen, Stan. *The Forgotten War*. Vol. 1. Missoula, Montana: Pictorial Histories Publishing, 1981.

———, *The Forgotten War*. Vol. 3. Missoula, Montana: Pictorial Histories Publishing, 1992.

Craven, Westley J., and James L. Cate. *The Army Air Forces in World War II*. Vol. 7, chap. 6, "Northwest Air Route to Alaska." Chicago: University of Chicago Press, 1958.

Deane, John R. *The Strange Alliance*. New York: Viking, 1947.

Garfield, Brian. *The Thousand-Mile War*. New York: Doubleday, 1969.

Gibson, James R. *Imperial Russia in Frontier America*. New York: Oxford University Press, 1976.

Goetzmann, William H., and Kay Sloan. *Looking Far North.* New York: Viking, 1982.

Goldenberg, L. A., and James L. Smith (ed.). *Gvozdev: The Russian Discovery of Alaska in 1732.* Anchorage: White Stone Press, 1990.

Hardesty, Von. *Red Phoenix: The Rise of Soviet Air Power, 1941–1945.* Washington: Smithsonian Institution Press, 1991.

Harriman, W. Averill, and Elie Abel. *Special Envoy to Churchill and Stalin, 1941–1946.* New York: Random House, 1975.

Hays, Otis, Jr. *Home from Siberia: The Secret Odysseys of Interned American Airmen in World War II.* College Station: Texas A&M University Press, 1990.

Herring, George C., Jr. *Aid to Russia, 1941–1946.* New York: Columbia University Press, 1973.

Higham, Robin, and Jacob W. Kipp. *Soviet Aviation and Air Power: A Historical View.* Boulder, Colo.: Westview Press, 1977.

Hough, Richard. *The Fleet That Had to Die.* New York: Viking, 1958.

Hunt, William R. *Arctic Passage.* New York: Scribner's, 1975.

Jones, Robert H. *The Roads to Russia: United States Lend-Lease to the Soviet Union.* Norman: University of Oklahoma Press, 1969.

Jordan, George R. *From Major Jordan's Diaries.* New York: Harcourt Brace, 1952.

Kennan, George. *Tent Life in Siberia.* Salt Lake City: Peregrine Smith Books, 1986.

Ketchum, Richard M. *Will Rogers, His Life and Times.* New York: American Heritage, 1973.

Langdon, Steve J. *The Native People of Alaska.* Anchorage: Greatland Graphics, 1987.

Lengyel, Emil. *Siberia.* Garden City, N.Y.: Garden City Publishing Co., 1943.

Len'kov, V. D., G. L. Silant'ev, and A. K. Staniukovich. *The Komandorskii Camp of the Bering Expedition.* Anchorage: Alaska Historical Society, 1992.

Lincoln, W. Bruce. *Conquest of a Continent.* New York: Random House, 1994.

Lindberg, Anne Morrow. *North to the Orient.* New York: Harcourt Brace, 1935.

Long, Everett A., and Ivan Y. Neganblya. *Cobras over the Tundra.* Fairbanks, Alaska: Arktika Publishing, 1992.

Lukas, Richard C. *Eagles East: The Army Air Force and the Soviet Union, 1941–1945.* Tallahassee: Florida State University Press, 1970.

Miller, David Hunter. *The Alaska Treaty.* Kingston, Ont., Canada: Limestone Press, 1981.

Muller, Gerhard Friedrich. *Bering's Voyages: The Reports from Russia*. Fairbanks: University of Alaska Press, 1986.

Pierce, Richard A. *Russian America: A Biographical Dictionary*. Kingston, Ont., Canada: Limestone Press, 1990.

Schwartz, Harry. *Tsars, Mandarins and Commissars*. Garden City, N.Y.: Doubleday, 1973.

Shelikhov, Grigorii I. *A Voyage to America, 1783–1786*. Kingston, Ont., Canada: Limestone Press, 1981.

Spector, Ronald H. *Eagle against the Sun*. New York: Free Press, 1985.

Standley, William H., and Arthur A. Agcton. *Admiral Ambassador to Russia*. Washington: Regnery, 1955.

Stephan, John J. *The Kuril Islands: Russo-Japanese Frontier in the Pacific*. New York: Oxford University Press, 1974.

———. *The Russian Far East: A History*. Stanford, Calif.; Stanford University Press, 1994.

Tompkins, Stuart Ramsay. *Alaska, Promyshlennik and Sourdough*. Norman: University of Oklahoma Press, 1945.

Twichell, Heath. *Northwest Epic: The Building of the Alaska Highway*. New York: St. Martin's Press, 1992.

Unterberger, Betty M. *Intervention against Communism: Did the United States Try to Overthrow the Soviet Government, 1918–1920?* Texas A&M University Lecture Series. College Station: Texas A&M University, 1986.

Van Tuyll, Hubert P. *Feeding the Bear: American Aid to the Soviet Union, 1941–1945*. New York: Greenwood Press, 1989.

Wagner, Ray. *American Combat Planes*. Garden City, N.Y.: Doubleday, 1982.

Walker, Ernest P. *Alaska: America's Continental Frontier Outpost*. Washington: Smithsonian Institution, 1943.

Watson, Thomas J., Jr., and Peter Petre. *Father Son & Co*. New York: Bantam, 1990.

Willmott, H. P. *Empires in the Balance*. Annapolis: Naval Institute Press, 1982.

ARTICLES

Ault, Phillip H. "The (Almost) Russian-American Telegraph." *American Heritage* (June, 1975).

Black, Lydia T. "Creoles in Russian America." *Pacifica* (November, 1990).

Chechin, Oleg. "Rescue of a Soviet Navigator." *Soviet Life* (November, 1989).

Cole, Terrence. "The Bridge to Tomorrow." *Alaska History* (Fall, 1990).

Daugherty, Frank J. "Escape from Siberia." *Alaska* (July, 1971).

Fortier, Edward J. "The Death of Private John White." *Fairbanks (Alaska) Daily News-Miner* (July 17 and 24, 1988).

Hardesty, Von. "Soviets Blaze Sky Trail over Top of World." *Air & Space* (December, 1987–January, 1988).

Hays, Otis, Jr. "The Silent Years in Alaska." *Alaska Journal* (1986 anthology).

———. "White Star, Red Star." *Alaska Journal* (Summer, 1982).

Krekshin, Igor. "TransSiberian Railway, Yesterday, Today, Tomorrow." *Russian Life* and *RIA Novesti Moscow* (Summer, 1994).

Liapunova, Rose G. "Aleuts before Contact with the Russians: Some Demographic and Cultural Aspects." *Pacifica* (November, 1990).

Mazuruk, Ilya. "Alaska-Siberia Airlift." *Soviet Life* (October, 1979).

Mazuruk, Maj. Gen. Ilya, Lt. Gen. Michael Machin, Maj. Gen. Mark Shevelev, Capt. Peter Gamov, Maj. Fyodor Zheviakov, Capt. Victor Perov, Capt. Dmitri Ostrovenko, and Capt. David Sherl. "Let's Meet Again!" *Soviet Life* (April, 1988).

Peterson, Steven M. "Russian Building Traditions and Their Legacy in Alaska." *Pacifica* (November, 1990).

Sardy, Mari. "Early Contact between Aleuts and Russians 1741–1780." *Alaska History* (Fall–Winter, 1985).

Sherl, David. "Alaska-Chukotka-Front, the Airlift That Never Failed." *Soviet Life* (December, 1986).

Solka, Paul. "Rescuing a Russian from the Wilderness." *Fairbanks (Alaska) Daily News-Miner* (March 10, 1984).

DOCUMENTS

Alaska Defense Command G-2 Russian Information Reports, February, 1943–May, 1943. Record Group 407, National Archives, Washington, D.C.

Alaska Defense Command/Alaskan Department Annexes to G-2 Periodic Reports, May, 1943–November, 1945. Record Group 338. National Archives, Washington, D.C.

Alaska Defense Command CI-R1 Summary Military Intelligence Report. "Pvt. John Oliver White, ASN 39950081, 83rd Depot Supply Squadron, Ladd Field, Alaska, 14 August 1943." Record Group 338. National Archives, Washington, D.C.

Alaskan Department Historical Report (undated draft). "Lend Lease Ferry Program." Record Group 338. National Archives, Washington, D.C.

Alaskan Department G-2 Summary (draft). "Notes on Valeri Tihonovich Minakov and His Escape from the USSR." Author's files.

Alaskan Division, Air Transport Command Historical Record Report. Vol. 2, chap. 8, "Early Ferrying Activities on the Northwest Route." Record Group 018, File 306.01. U.S. Air Force Historical Research Center, Maxwell Air Force Base, Alabama.

Alaskan Division, Air Transport Command Historical Record Report. Vol. 2, chap. 9, "Organization of the Northwest Ferrying Route." Record Group 018, File 306.01. U.S. Air Force Historical Research Center, Maxwell Air Force Base, Alabama.

Alaskan Division, Air Transport Command Historical Record Report. Vol. 2, "1944 Operations." Record Group 018, File 306.01. U.S. Air Force Historical Research Center, Maxwell Air Force Base, Alabama.

Carr, Edwin R. "History of the Northwest Air Route to Alaska, 1942–45." Record Group 018, File 306.01. U.S. Air Force Historical Research Center, Maxwell Air Force Base, Alabama.

Deane, John R. "Report of the Commanding General, United States Military Mission to Moscow, October 18, 1943–October 31, 1945." Record Group 334, National Archives, Washington, D.C.

Pearson, Drew. "Washington Merry-Go-Round." (Syndicated newspaper column released Sept. 16, 1943). Lyndon Baines Johnson Library archives, Austin, Texas.

Index

Detachment, 60. *See also* I&I Russian section

I&I Russian section, 61–62, 63, 70, 99, 110

I&I Soviet escorts, 61, 115–16, 117–18, 119–20, 123–25

Jones, Edwin W., 26, 75, 76, 92, 95, 97, 102, 115

Jordan, George R., 138–39

Keillor, Russell, 58, 82, 83

Kiselev, Peter S., 40, 77, 90, 94, 105, 106, 109

Kiseleva, Maria, 95

Kisevalter, George G., 62, 63, 99, 135–36

Kitchingman, Raymond F., 35, 36, 37, 39, 45

Kodiak Naval Air Station, 18, 19–20, 121–22

Komar, Makary F., 40, 80–84, 170

Komar, Mark I., 83, 172

Krolicki, Thaddius, 61

Kwantung Army, 15, 16, 122, 130

Ladd Field (Fairbanks), 133; commanders at, 49, 58, 131; construction of, 12; facilities at, 35, 80; and Lend Lease transfer point, 30, 38. *See also* ALSIB route; Northwest route

Langer, William, 94

"leaders of fighters," 54

Lend-Lease, 127; aircraft of, 56, 86; protocols of, 23, 28, 49, 50, 57, 78, 96, 102, 105, 110, 111, 113, 122; supply routes of, 23–24, 26–27. *See also* ALSIB route; Northwest route

Lend-Lease Act: and ALSIB Lend-Lease, 131; legislation passed by, 14; and Soviet aid debate, 14, 15; and Soviets, 23; Stalin's praise of, 113; and U.S.-Soviet alliance, 27. *See also* Lend-Lease, supply routes of

Levitsky, Vsevolod, 71, 142

liaison: as foreign, 60; problems with, 25, 59, 72, 74, 75, 80–84, 96, 97, 101. *See also* I&I Russian section

liaison officers: as permanent, 65–66, 68, 70, 99, 117; as temporary, 61

linguists, Russian, 60

Litvinov, Maxime, 28

Machin, Michael G., 40, 78, 79, 83, 84, 90, 95, 96–97, 108–109, 137, 140

Madievsky, Anatole, 67, 130

Makarova, Elena A., 40, 43–44, 85, 109, 138, 171

Maksutov, Dmitrii, 7–8

Marks Field (Nome), 36, 49, 58, 76

Mazuruk, Ilya P., 31, 32, 55–56, 87, 105, 126, 137, 140

Mihailov, Vassily, 71

Minakov, Valeri, 128–29, 138

Molokov, V., 26

Molotov, V. M., 28, 112, 124

monuments, war memorial (ALSIB), 140

Mosley, Thomas, 50, 57

Muraviev, Nikolai, 6–7

Nedosekin, Pavel, 45

Nicholas II (czar), 8, 9

Nome army, 36; commanders of, 115; garrison of, 35

Nome ATC, 58; commanders of, 131; service organization of, 49, 104. *See also* Marks Field

Nome Soviet garrison, 52, 92, 102, 171

Northwest route, 35–36, 56; aircraft at, 131, 167; conditions of bases at, 33, 49–50, 58, 104; first Lend-Lease delivery at, 39, 44; organization of, 34, 50–51, 56–58, 80, 104, 105, 113; weather conditions on, 38, 48

Northwest Staging Route, xi; map of 34. *See also* Northwest route

Obrazkov, Ivan A., 128

Paul I (czar), 5. *See also* Russian American Company